Toward Better Problems

IN THE SERIES ETHICS AND ACTION

EDITED BY TOM REGAN

Toward Better Problems

New Perspectives on Abortion, Animal Rights, the Environment, and Justice

ANTHONY WESTON

TEMPLE UNIVERSITY PRESS *Philadelphia*

Temple University Press, Philadelphia 19122
Copyright © 1992 by Temple University. All rights reserved
Published 1992
Printed in the United States of America

Library of Congress Cataloging-in-Publication Data

Weston, Anthony, 1954–
    Toward better problems : new perspectives on abortion, animal
rights, the environment, and justice / Anthony Weston.
        p.   cm. — (Ethics and action)
    Includes bibliographical references and index.
    ISBN 0–87722–947–3 (cloth : alk. paper). — ISBN 0–87722–948–1
(pbk. : alk. paper)
    1. Social ethics. 2. Social problems. 3. United States—Social
conditions—1980–   I. Title. II. Series.
HM216.W43   1992
303.3′72—dc20   91-38507

Contents

v

Preface

THE STUDY of ethics in American universities today is almost always a study of ethical theories. Every well-trained student has heard of John Stuart Mill's Utilitarianism, Kant's Categorical Imperative, and Aristotle's Doctrine of the Mean. By contrast, the idea that ethics might not necessarily be exhausted by, or even well represented by, the analysis and application of such theories remains a virtual heresy.

Yet the heresy is spreading. A number of writers in feminist ethics have begun to insist not merely on an ethics of "care" and relationship as opposed to the more distant and impersonal ethics of justice, but also on a reconception of the very nature of practical ethics. Carol Gilligan depicts a kind of ethical thinking that arises and responds within specific situations and lifestories rather than trying to fit such situations and stories into a general framework of moral rules.[1] Margaret Walker argues that ethics is not a science or a kind of puzzle solving but instead "a collection of perceptive, imaginative, appreciative, and expressive skills and capacities which put us and keep us in contact with the realities of ourselves and specific others."[2] Virginia Warren speaks of the need to rethink and change the problems themselves. Rather than asking what to do with a comatose patient whose wishes regarding euthanasia her doctors do not know, for example, we might pay more attention to why her doctors don't know, or why no one bothered to find out. Warren proposes, perhaps acidly, to call such an inquiry "preventive ethics."[3]

Challenging the current assumptions from another direction, Albert Jonsen and Stephen Toulmin have begun to rehabilitate casuistry, a persistent tradition of moral reasoning well developed and widely used from antiquity through the seventeenth century. Casuists explicitly rejected what Jonsen and Toulmin call "moral geometry": the view that moral questions are to be resolved by deducing the answers from fixed first principles.[4] Instead they advanced a "network" of more concrete considerations and analogies, establishing presumptions rather than certainties. They were experts at what Aristotle called *phronesis,* "practical wisdom."

Developments within "official" ethics are not so sanguine for theory either. Bernard Williams, in his aptly titled book *Ethics and the Limits of Philosophy,* contends that the theoretical project in ethics has no justification and should be abandoned. He urges instead a more "holistic" approach, whose aim is to "show how a given [value] hangs together with other [values] in ways that make social and psychological sense."[5] The new ethics of "virtue," meanwhile, also rejects fixed rules and principles, paralleling the feminist critics, and makes a systematic project of reconstituting *phronesis.*[6]

So it is a time of ferment at the frontiers of ethics. Still, however, the standard ethics course plows the same old furrows. Practical ethics in particular remains an affair of applying theories to specific problems. It remains "applied ethics," and thus a direct descendant of the "moral geometry" rejected by all of the critics just cited. But it is not hard to understand why moral geometry has such staying power. It may seem necessary, especially in practice-minded courses, to stick to the one kind of practice that is now well developed, at least until a comparably substantial body of practical work emerges from the new critiques. As yet the critiques remain mostly reactive, as is Williams's book, or historical, like Jonsen and Toulmin's, or theoretical in a different mode, as are the virtue theories. By and large, an alternative practical ethics has yet to emerge.

This book aims to offer such a practical ethics. Insofar as there is at least a rough convergence among all the critics just cited—toward a less rule-bound practice, more sensitive both to a variety of ethical skills and to a variety of relevant values, and toward a "preventive" sort of ethics that engages ethical problems over time rather than regarding them as "puzzles" to be solved—this book's method stands at that convergence. But this book is emphatically not a kind of summation of critiques that would thus stand at an even greater distance from the actual problems of ethics. Instead it turns in the opposite direction: it focuses almost immediately on practical issues. It aims to outline a kind of practice that can exemplify, complete, and make approachable the emerging critique(s) of philosophical ethics as we know it. I want to offer a developed model of an alternative.[7]

To do so, however, this book takes its methodological starting point and chief inspiration from a source not yet mentioned, and indeed strikingly underrated by the current criticisms of traditional ethics. I begin with the pragmatic tradition, especially as exemplified in the ethical method developed in a number of works by John Dewey.

Pragmatism and ethics may seem an odd combination. Popularly, at least, the term "pragmatism" suggests a kind of self-serving or pedestrian amorality, or at least a lack of any fixed principles. Dewey's pragmatism, however, actually bears only the most distant of relations to this stereotype, and in some ways bears no relation at all. Dewey means us to embrace the richness and diversity of our actual values and then to make full use of that richness and diversity to open up a new sense of possibility and flexibility in practical action. Pragmatism, so understood, represents a pluralistic, integrative, even experimental approach to ethics, at once an almost ordinary kind of practical wisdom and a philosophically self-conscious alternative in ethics.

I believe, then, that Dewey has already opened the space for the kind of "alternative" ethical practice that is now necessary. We may bring to bear the resources of an established philosophical tradition to begin to undergird and inspire a broader, more pluralistic, and more inventive kind of ethical practice than we are currently offered. The casuists' value-networking *phronesis,* for example, parallels the Deweyan project of integrating or harmonizing values. Warren's notion of "preventive" ethics echoes the Deweyan notion of "social reconstruction": both suggest that we try to change social conditions so that certain problematic situations do not even arise, or arise in a more tractable form. In short, I believe that we can take the most contemporary of steps forward at the same time as we reinvoke and reinvigorate a philosophical approach too often relegated to the status of historical curiosity. We might say instead that Dewey was just ahead of his time. Only now are we ready for him.

An immediate caveat: I do not claim that my suggestions represent the only possible "Deweyan" views, let alone the only possible "pragmatic" ethic. Lovejoy distinguished no less than thirteen different types of pragmatism, and Dewey alone has been read in a multitude of different ways. I offer only one Dewey, one pragmatism. Indeed, for Dewey specialists I probably should add that I hardly even offer one Dewey. It should already be clear that my main aim is not exegetical. The aim is simply to think in a Deweyan way, to engage contemporary issues in practical ethics in a way inspired by Dewey's work, not to insist on his terms or even on his particular views of the issues addressed.

Mine is not a particularly fashionable Dewey, either. In particular, I am not concerned to recast pragmatism as a mode of deconstructive cultural criticism, though I have learned from the work of philosophers who have. The Dewey who inspires this book is directly engaged with specific social and moral problems. Far from being less challenging, those problems pose, in my view, the most challenging tasks of all. Far from being less "scholarly"—should that be someone's concern—engaging them seems to me to be one of the most appropriate of scholarly tasks. It could not be more unfortunate or unpromising, either for society or for scholarship, when the actual problems of our collective life are not regarded as "of scholarly interest."

Another caveat: what follows is not necessarily the sort of practice that Jonsen and Toulmin, Walker, Warren, or Williams ideally have in mind. It is not exactly casuistical, for instance, because it is at least as interested in transforming or reconstructing problems as it is in "solving" them. I do believe that my pragmatism is at least congruent with most of the critical views I have cited—and where I think this congruence is especially clear, and where these somewhat more metaethical topics are appropriate, I make some connections—but in general this book is no more meant as an exact account of what the critics might have in mind than it is meant as an exact account of Dewey's views. Instead, again, it is an attempt to speak for an overlooked but immensely suggestive tradition by *exemplifying* that tradition, in accord with its own constructive tendencies, in contemporary practice.

One advantage of this practical focus is that it should make this book accessible to a wide range of readers. My hope is that it will prove useful to students of ethics at all levels, to professionals in related fields, and to all who are interested in the problems it addresses. I do presuppose some familiarity with a few basics of modern philosophical ethics, in particular with the general outlines of utilitarianism and rights theories. Still, I presuppose only a familiarity that may be picked up in an introductory ethics course or by intelligently reading the popular or professional literature in, say, business ethics, policy analysis, or bioethics. Philosophical jargon and offhand references are confined (I hope!) to this preface and to some of the notes.

Let me add just a few words about some issues of genuine importance and sustained interest to specialists that must be left out of this book. The last chapter briefly takes up a family of the most prominent and unavoidable objections to a pragmatic attitude. Other objections and theoretical issues are left for discussion elsewhere. This book does not, for example, offer a full-fledged theory of values to undergird and rationalize the styles of argument about values that I employ. Dewey and others have already done so.[8] Also, less fortunately, in the traditional terms a Deweyan value theory tends to fall into a philosophical category—"subjectivism"— that is persistently oversimplified and stereotyped, much like "pragmatism" itself, thus requiring still more time and space—probably an entire book—to make clear. Deweyan subjectivism, for the record, simply locates values in the complex social and biological articulation of human desire rather than in some independent realm of truths. That is all I mean when invoking "subjectivism" here. Much can then be said about just how this articulation proceeds and about the ways in which, by linking values together into networks of logical and motivational connections, it opens values to critical argument and change. It is certainly unfortunate that we do not yet have such a value-theoretic subjectivism fully worked out and available as a reference point for more practical studies such as this book. But we don't, and this is not the place to develop it.[9]

There are other exclusions that a heavier tome might avoid. I do not explore the theoretical congruences just sketched as fully as many might like. More could be said about the connections to casuistry or, say, to virtue theory, which shares pragmatism's rejections of fixed rules and principles and pragmatism's attention to context and a plurality of values, although (in my view) over-emphasizing individual character. But to do so would once again dilute the practical focus of this book and render it less accessible and less useful to those just beginning to think about ethics and to those coming to ethical inquiry from other fields. Thus only a little is said here about these connections, again mostly in the notes. Any more is out of place in a book intended for a wider audience, and in a book that attempts to keep the proof at least related to the pudding.

My main hope is actually very modest. I hope to begin to reanimate a certain style of thinking, a certain style of taking up problems, that is familiar and natural outside of ethics but seems to have lost its self-confidence and to some extent self-consciousness within ethics. Again, I am much more concerned to let this "attitude" emerge in practice, as a practical style of ethical thinking, than to fully characterize it theoretically and to advance it on the level of general philosophical arguments. The aim is not to launch a new dreadnought onto the philosophical waters. Think of this book instead as a set of proposals in a pragmatic spirit, meant for provocation and expecting revision. I sincerely hope that it proves useful.

Portions of Chapter 3 first appeared in my article "Drawing Lines: The Abortion Perplex and the Presuppositions of Applied Ethics," *Monist* 67 (1984): 589–604. Portions of Chapter 5 appeared in "Beyond Intrinsic Value: Pragmatism in Environmental Ethics," *Environmental Ethics* 7 (1985): 321–39. I am grateful to the editors of both journals for permission to reprint these passages here.

These thoughts began to coalesce into a book in a month spent on the Maine coast thanks to the generosity of the late Bettyann Sankar. Peter Williams and Jennifer Church read and reread drafts of the early chapters and filled the margins with comments that led me more than once to start over. Jay Hullet, Lee Miller, Eva Feder Kittay, and Amy Halberstadt were persistent in their encouragement and support of many kinds. Dorian Gregory, Kieran Suckling, and Shari Stone read large parts of the manuscript and contributed greatly to its clarity. For supporting their work with summer work-study grants I am grateful to the Department of Philosophy at SUNY–Stony Brook. As the project neared completion I was fortunate indeed for the generous critical support of Tom Regan and for the equally generous editorial support of Jane Cullen. I am indebted also to several anonymous readers. It is a pleasure and an honor to acknowledge the care and support that so many of my friends, students, and colleagues have given to this project.

Anthony Weston

Chapter 1

Practical Ethics in a New Key

MANY other "practical ethics" books take up the same topics as this one: abortion, other animals, the environment, justice. Peter Singer covers much the same ground in a book called simply *Practical Ethics*.[1]

The actual practicality of the usual brand of practical ethics, however, is somewhat partial. What we are usually offered is the systematic application of some ethical theory *to* practice. Singer's book represents an admirably lucid application of utilitarianism. Others apply theories of rights to the same set of issues. In both of these cases, the broad outlines of an ethical theory are assumed in advance. The principles employed are defended, at any rate against other principles, somewhere else. In practical ethics of this type, ethical theories are just put to work, without much ado about their origins or ultimate justification, to sort out practical questions. A few adjustments in the basic principles may be made to accommodate especially difficult or new practical problems, but by and large the principles are taken as given before the practical inquiry even starts. Principles dictate, practice adjusts—though of course practice may adjust with great subtlety and sensitivity.

In these well-known kinds of practical ethics, moreover, there is a natural tendency toward a certain kind of closure. The project is to sort out the practical questions at stake in a way that finally allows one or a few facts—one or a few kinds of issues, one or a few aspects of value—to determine the answer. The abortion issue, for example, may be reduced finally to a question of the rights of the fetus, and the question of the rights of the fetus may be reduced in turn to the question of when fetuses become "human beings." Suppose that fetuses become human beings at conception, for example, and an entire ethical position follows automatically. All that we need to work out are the details. Or again, if one starts with a principle like "Minimize suffering" (a variant of utilitarianism), then the ethical question about other animals becomes solely a question of whether and how they suffer. The answer to the further question whether the rest of nature has ethical standing in its own right can also be deduced at a stroke: it is no.

Looking for definitive answers in this sense may seem perfectly natural. The point of practical ethics, we say, is to figure out what actually to do. To figure out what to do, we say, we must settle on the most essential aspect or aspects of the problem, thus setting out the essential questions, questions whose answers yield a definite solution. This procedure seems even more natural if one's ethical thinking is anchored from the start in basic principles, which after all are meant precisely to allow certain aspects of ethical problems to determine our answers to them. This kind of appeal to principles is what has been called the "classical tradition" in practical ethics.[2] It is certainly not the only tradition—actually it is not even "classical," in the sense of being the most ancient or time-honored—but it is certainly the tradition we know best, and for many of us is the only one we know at all.

It is possible, however, to take up practical problems in a radically different spirit, a spirit associated in particular with the work of the American pragmatist John Dewey. This book is an attempt to do so. In this book I do *not* propose new "solutions" to the old problems to put alongside the two or five plausible principle-based solutions already debated in the literature. Nor do I propose a new set of ethical principles to put alongside the familiar utilitarianisms and theories of rights. I am not concerned with rearranging the contours of the familiar problems so that somewhat different dimensions determine a somewhat new set of answers. Instead, I have pursued two rather different general strategies.

First, in engaging practical issues I aim to draw out their complexity, to view them from multiple sides and on many levels. I will *resist* taking one or a few dimensions of a problem to alone determine an ethical response. I will insist that ethical problems are seldom "puzzles," allowing specific and conclusive "solutions." Instead I will treat them as larger and vaguer regions of tension, requiring very different strategies in response. In addition I will regularly ask how we ended up in a situation where these particular kinds of difficulties emerge as problems in the first place. "The" problems as first presented are not taken as sacrosanct, and they may end up still more complex once viewed in social and historical perspective.

This may hardly seem practical. One may certainly wonder how making a problem still more complex contributes to solving it. Part of my answer will be that "solutions" in the contemporary sense are not exactly what we should seek. We *are* concerned, in the pragmatic spirit, with effective and intelligent action in the present and with progressive change in the future. But viewing problems in a more complex and multi-sided way, I will argue, is actually a means to those ends. By keeping our conception of a problem many-sided and flexible, we begin to make ethical thinking a process of engagement rather than a more episodic kind of problem solving. In such an ongoing process there is more room for inventiveness, experiment, and imagination. It will be understood that the problem allows many different approaches and that their promise cannot be known a priori. Moreover, by inquiring into the social and historical roots of ethical problems, we open the possibility of transforming "the" problem itself into something more manageable. This project Dewey called "reconstruction," and it will be a central theme in this book.

Second, in engaging the values at stake in such problems, the approach in this book will be "integrative." Rather than trying to define certain dimensions of value as determinative, overriding others, the project here is to engage and sort out a complex and conflicting set of values from *within:* to try to clarify their dynamics without simplifying them, and to suggest ways to rearrange and better integrate some of the less clear values while still honoring their place within the whole.

The book's expectation, then, is not that we can find a single definitive strand within the fabric of our values, but instead that we must work with and within the larger pattern of values itself, as a whole. The pragmatic project so conceived can thus be linked to "holistic" epistemologies developed in twentieth-century analytic philosophy, partly themselves in the pragmatic spirit. Holistic arguments appeal not to one kind of supposedly determinative consideration but instead to the interrelations and mutual reinforcement of a complex set of beliefs or values. As Bernard Williams puts it, the aim is "to show how a given [value] hangs together with other [values] in a way that makes social and psychological sense."[3] We are invited not to "ground" all values by reference to one or a few specific kinds of consideration, but instead to offer a kind of accounting or "location" of particular values in their contexts, to place them within rich and ongoing processes.

The method is difficult to describe in general without resorting to metaphors, such as Williams's "hanging together" and even "holism" itself. Dewey wrote evocatively but not so informatively of "the moving unbalanced balance of things." Although holistic notions recur regularly in the contemporary criticism of the familiar principle-based ethics, the actual workings of holism remain relatively unexplored. This is one reason why this book turns so persistently to practice. One of its aims is to offer a proposal about how holism in ethics might actually look.

Even after more elaboration, integrative and reconstructive methods may be hard to recognize as ethical methods at all, considering their contrast to more familiar forms of practical ethics. On the other hand, I also believe that pragmatic attitudes toward problems—just plain problems, so long as they are not classified as "ethical"—are not at all unfamiliar. We may not always manage to think so imaginatively or integratively about our practical problems, but—again, outside of ethics—we at least have some sense of the appropriateness of such strategies. In a sense, then, it might be argued that pragmatism represents only a reinvocation and reanimation within ethics of an approach to problems that does not surprise anyone when it is advanced in other regions of life. There we need to learn to apply it better. In ethics we need, in the first place, simply to learn to apply it.

Chapter 2

Pragmatic Attitudes

THE MOST general introduction to pragmatic ethics would start with a view of the universe and of the place of human values in it. Dewey paints a picture of human beings as co-evolved parts of a complex natural order, in which "value" is not some special property that enters the natural world only through the grace of God or the discernment of the wise, but exists already, in profusion, all around us. Value is a form of desire; desire is a form of attraction common to all living things; living things are incomplete beings needing both sustenance and growth, subject to constant uncertainty but also stimulated and fulfilled at the same time by the struggles that uncertainty and need impose on us.[1]

But these themes require a very large canvas, and there is no such space here. We must begin with a particular part of the picture: with a pragmatic, and again specifically Deweyan, view of the nature of ethical *problems*. In any specific choice, Dewey would remind us, there are a large number of interests and aims—both one's own and others'—at stake. Some will be incompatible. Some we will trust, or come to trust, more than others. Some will matter more or differently than others. Correspondingly, there will be a variety of different possibilities for action, and in each case a fairly delicate balancing act may be necessary. Ethical problems are not at all neat, then, and there is no guarantee that they have neat answers. It is not obvious that they require anything like the rigorous application of principles. Some may not even be tractable. In short, on Dewey's view, the real problems of ethics are very different from the problems we are usually offered. The implications for ethical method, correspondingly, may be quite radical.

From Puzzles to Problematic Situations

Let us begin with just this question: What exactly *is* an ethical problem? Examples of ethical problems are familiar enough: issues that arise in medical contexts, for example euthanasia and abortion; issues about the environment and other animals; issues about honesty in public office and private relationships; and so on. What these "problems" themselves are, however—what kind of difficulty they actually represent—is not at all so obvious. There is a world of difference between the kind of problem represented by a crossword puzzle and the kind of problem represented by an uncooperative child. Utterly different strategies are necessary. Consequently, then, one of the fundamental tasks of any systematic ethical philosophy is to investigate the nature of ethical problems themselves. Knowing a list of examples, however familiar they may be, is no guarantee that we know what kinds of problems they are examples *of.*

We might begin by distinguishing two fundamentally different kinds of problems. "Puzzles," on the one hand, are fairly discrete and self-contained difficulties or challenges. They do not require us to address large sets of related issues at the same time. Correspondingly, puzzles also have definite and specific solutions. They promise a definitive and verifiable, right or wrong answer, even if we have not yet arrived at it.

Brainteasers and crossword puzzles are obvious examples of puzzles. So are many mathematical problems, not just because they can be stated in very precise ways but also because all of us acquired, early on, the habit of regarding mathematical problems as definitively solvable—though in fact some are not. Murder mysteries are another example. One knows from the start that there is a villain or villains and thus that a "solution" to the mystery exists and will be demonstrated in the end.

Puzzles, though, are only one kind of problem. What Dewey called "problematic situations" are an entirely different kind of problem. Problematic situations are problems that are not discrete and self-contained but instead arise out of larger patterns of life and practice, so that even to speak of "the" problem is somewhat misleading. Often the best we can do is vaguely indicate a region of social tension or individual discomfort, areas of confusion or distress. Such feelings are only the natural consequence when creatures with varied and even conflicting needs and values encounter situations that are themselves rich in possibilities. Correspondingly, though, problematic situations have no definite and specific solutions, no conclusively right answers. We will seldom be able to satisfy every desire or actualize every promising possibility of a situation. It is not a matter of finding a single key to unlock a recalcitrant lock. Instead we must speak in terms of general strategies, approaches, even attitudes, and only indirectly of "solving" a problem at all. As a matter of course we expect sustained engagement rather than conclusive resolutions.[2]

I do not mean that problematic situations are in any way special. Indeed, I will later suggest that they, not puzzles, are the norm. Consider the case of tensions between friends or co-workers. Occasionally such tensions have a very specific cause, maybe even a single misunderstanding, that can be cleared away at a stroke once it is figured out. If so, then what seemed to be a problematic situation was really only a puzzle. But this is also exceedingly rare, although some of us nonetheless approach interpersonal tensions as if there were always a single and simple way back to good feeling. Usually the tension is much more deeply rooted. Interests may conflict by the nature of the tasks involved at work; personal inclinations and styles may rankle others; outside pressures may intensify personal disagreements. Usually the only constructive way through is a slow reopening of communication, painstaking reestablishment of trust, a range of symbolic and substantive moves to address the sources of tension. Sometimes progress will be faster than at other times, but in general it is a *process,* a struggle, with no single decisive moment.

Situations that are problematic in this way can be very personal—patterns of dependency, for instance, or "writer's block"—or they may be social and large scale, like the state of American education. Regardless of their scale, however, all problematic situations have certain similar features. A multiplicity of values are at stake (in education, for example, the values of knowledge, socialization, autonomy, discipline, creativity, etc.); not all of these values are likely to be fully attainable at the same time; past attempts at keeping them in some kind of balance seem to have failed, though the history of these attempts has important lessons to teach; and our present attempts to do better may well prove inadequate in various ways in turn, perhaps as conditions change, and will eventually become part of the history of the problematic situation too. Exploration and experiment are invited—in fact, are required. We can only expect a long struggle, though not without its rewards and occasional breakthroughs.

Ethical Problems as Puzzles

Since I teach ethics, I am often approached for ethical advice, though my training as an ethical philosopher never encompassed or apparently even envisioned the prospect. But it does give me an opportunity to see what people ordinarily expect ethical advice to be like. And the first and most consistent expectation is that ethical problems are fairly discrete and self-contained, and correspondingly that they have specific and definite answers, even "right" answers. Popularly, at least, ethical problems are supposed to be puzzles.

Students ask my advice about honesty in their relationships. If A is regularly dating B, can A also date C without telling B? Students really do put the question just this abstractly, as if they really have been persuaded that the particulars of their situation have nothing to do with the answer. And consistently, despite the novelty and complexity of the situations that give rise to their questions, students expect to be told either "yes" or "no." What they do not expect, and often do not quite understand or appreciate, is more process-oriented advice, like "Talk to B about your relationship." They want answers, solutions, and they think that all the facts are in.

Nurses express concern about the reserve they feel when caring for patients with highly infectious and poorly understood diseases. Is it fair to the patient to offer less care, more "distant" care, than they would with other patients? Is it fair to themselves not to hold back? Again, though, they ask *me*, not their co-workers or their patients themselves. It is not just that putting such questions to their patients themselves might seem unprofessional, and not just that the unwritten etiquette of the hospital may discourage raising these questions with co-workers. They also really believe that these are matters they must sort out for themselves, and that definitive answers can be found in the privacy of their own deliberations.[3] When stumped, then, they go to a (supposed!) expert, thus perpetuating the notion that there is a right answer to be found, even when they no longer trust themselves to find it.

Philosophers in practical ethics are only a little more circumspect about taking the familiar problems to have solutions. Many philosophical treatments of the abortion issue, for example, take as their goal the defense of a particular "line" in fetal development before which abortions are allowable and after which they are not.[4] "The" issue is again supposed to be fairly specific, to have definite outlines, and to be resolvable by conceptual analysis. Or again, Peter Singer concludes *Animal Liberation* by telling us exactly what we can and cannot eat. Such approaches in practical ethics can of course reveal new and overlooked dimensions of problems. I shall read Singer in exactly this way in Chapter 4. Still, this is not the spirit in which practical ethics such as his are actually offered. The aim and expectation is closure: to be able to say "yes" or "no" or "do it this way" rather than to give advice like "negotiate" or "talk to B about it."

Consider also our *pattern* of attention to ethical issues. Too often our attention is temporary and episodic, even impatient. "If only they would get married," or "If only abortion were illegal," or "If only we could figure out whether capital punishment is constitutional." Ethical problems are supposed to be restricted and specific, hence puzzles, rather than general and persistent, like problematic situations. Ethical problems become a little like diseases, making ethics analogous to acute-care medicine, which may be why medical ethics has seemed so natural a development. Correspondingly, just as we are not inclined to pay much attention to unhealthy features of our overall life situations so long as we are feeling fairly healthy at the moment, we are disinclined to pay attention to the deeper and more persistent problems in our personal or societal situations until they emerge in the unavoidable questions that we do recognize as ethical problems. If we really are made to face the deeper problems, we are more apt to think of the task as "therapy" than as "ethics"—not recognizing in therapy itself a form of ethical engagement.

Likewise, much of the philosophical literature in practical ethics restricts itself not merely to concrete problems but also to specific *episodic* problems. In fact, this self-restriction seems virtually to define the idea of practical ethics, at least insofar as it is contrasted with ethical theory. The paradigmatic problems are "episodes" or "cases," to which theories are to be "applied," as for example a paradigm case with respect to euthanasia.

> V is the victim of a traffic accident, now deep in a coma in the Intensive Care Unit and wholly dependent on life support. Short-term survival is likely with help, but brain damage is almost certain and even the return of consciousness is unlikely. V's family is traumatized but may be willing to accept her death. What should be done?[5]

Such cases are stock examples in most bioethics courses. Moreover, once again, these sorts of problems are usually supposed to have at most two or three possible answers. Here the usual answers would be to keep V going, or to remove life support and let her die forthwith, or perhaps to remove life support slowly and only when her family is more prepared. Each answer can appeal to its appropriate principles. Each is fairly simple, both to "justify" and to carry out. Again, then, such cases, however gripping and tragic and difficult, are at bottom still supposed to be puzzles.[6]

Ethical Problems as Problematic Situations

I will argue, by contrast, for the Deweyan view that ethical problems are typically "problematic situations." Even at their most specific, ethical problems are best understood as points of emergence of deeper patterns of values in tension, and correspondingly must be engaged in a much more flexible and extended way. Indeed, on this view, the episodic posing of yes-or-no questions is a radical distortion of the true requirements of ethical thinking.

Consider again young people worrying about honesty in their relationships. Instead of taking "the" problem to be simply finding the right ethical principles to apply, a first move might be to ask why such worries arise in the first place. Part of the reason is surely that intimate relationships are relatively new in young people's lives. It is no surprise that uncertainties and questions arise. Recognizing this background, however, also makes it imperative to answer their questions in a way that encourages some self-reflection and growth rather than simply delivering a verdict (even if one could). For example, one might point out that honesty is not a remote kind of value that enters our lives only on formal occasions. Patterns of trust and mistrust are built up and defined in a relationship over time, imperceptibly growing from the small and occasionally large choices the partners make. So I ask: What patterns and expectations of yours—not of some abstract "A" or "B," but *yours*—are already established in your relationships? Have they proved to be constructive patterns? If not, how could they be changed?

Notice that the explicit and prolonged attention in counseling and therapy is precisely to such patterns. No therapist worth her salt would view problems of intimacy and honesty as episodes to be simply resolved, one way or another, and then put aside. A tendency to reduce such issues to episodes might even be the root of the difficulty. This does not mean that there is nothing to say about the specific question that presents itself now. But it does mean, as I shall suggest throughout this book, that what we might say is quite different from "yes" or "no."

Again also, problematic situations involve a multiplicity of values. Consider, for a larger-scale example, the issue of euthanasia, as posed by the familiar philosophical cases such as the case of V. The usual approach in practical ethics is to distinguish two basic principles supposed to be at stake: the principle of autonomy, which makes an individual's free choice the final arbiter for all matters concerning her life and health, and the principle of beneficence, which enjoins us always to serve the patient's own good. "The" problem is supposed to be that in many cases these two principles conflict. Beneficence sometimes suggests that it would be better for a person to be allowed to die, but the patient's own preferences may be unobtainable, or she may have been opposed to euthanasia. Conversely, some patients may clearly request to be allowed to die, while their doctors may feel that beneficence—considering the patient's own good in the long run—requires saving their lives.[7]

Two different and not entirely consistent dimensions of value are present in this case. Presumably their co-presence is supposed to be a *conflict* because we insist on defining problems in terms of principles that allow such problems to be "solved." Principles at odds do not yield definitive solutions. From a pragmatic point of view, however, the mere co-presence of different dimensions of value is not necessarily a "conflict" at all. The effect may instead be only to remind us, once again, that our values tend to be complicated, that many concerns must be addressed at once. A multiplicity of values may be irreducible. Many "bioethicists" themselves, having given up on elevating one of these principles above the other, will speak instead of "balancing" them in particular cases. Pragmatism simply suggests a different metaphor for this already-acknowledged process. Instead of the head-on collision of different frames of values, we have multiple dimensions of value that must learn how to cooperate.

Moreover, the dimensions of value at stake here hardly stop with two. Many other values are also involved. Bodily integrity is important in its own right, for example; thus the degree of invasiveness of the life-support measures being used is relevant. As those measures become more invasive, the clearer and stronger the need for them must be. Or again, utilitarian considerations, for example other possible uses of the sometimes staggering medical resources consumed in keeping hopeless cases alive, also enter the picture. I do not mean that these considerations are decisive—they are no more decisive than any other single kind of consideration—but they do represent another dimension of what by now we must recognize to be a very complex story. Nor should there be any compulsion to somehow reduce these further dimensions to the original supposed conflict between autonomy and beneficence: reducing the question of bodily integrity, for instance, to an aspect of a person's general "well-being," considered under the heading of beneficence. The invitation is to set aside the "collision" model of the situation, not to reinforce it, or, by assuming it in advance, to make it self-fulfilling.

Given a problematic situation such as the case of V, then, the pragmatic task is not at all a matter of elevating one principle over another that conflicts with it. Instead it is a matter of understanding and articulating the multiplicity of values involved and beginning to negotiate some jointly acceptable policies. Naturally this is a much less tidy and decisive approach than the "solutions" for which we are now encouraged to aim. Even to illustrate it adequately will take most of this book. The above sketch is only the barest outline. But perhaps at least this much is clear: the search for "solutions" misrepresents and distorts the actual situation. If it is a problematic situation and not a puzzle, then an untidy and open-ended approach is the only appropriate one.

Caveats

I do not mean that *all* ethical problems are problematic situations. Certain ethical problems may well be more like puzzles. Sometimes, for instance, only one or a few values are involved. Sometimes certain values are clearly more important than others. But of course cases of these sorts are not likely to emerge as ethical problems in the first place. There are also some cases that do emerge as ethical problems in which clearer thinking can truly establish one dimension of values as decisive. But of course cases of these sorts are not likely to remain ethical problems.

The familiar problems do remain. Some regularly recur. Others recur in new forms: issues of life and death; social goals versus individual claims; fairness; the very right to ethical attention in the first place. Equally clearheaded people come to opposite conclusions. *Really* clearheaded people may come to no conclusion at all. From the fact that a few ethical problems turn out to be puzzles, then, it does not follow that all the rest are only more recalcitrant puzzles. They may be a different kind of problem entirely. In fact the puzzles may be the special cases, highly specified situations in which, improbably, a "solution" actually is possible.

One can buy books of chess puzzles, contrived situations in which a specific solution—say, unavoidable checkmate in three moves—is necessary. Elaborate computer programs exist to make sure that only one such solution is possible and that there is no unexpected way out. But from puzzles of this sort it certainly does not follow that all chess problems are only more complex versions of the same thing. In fact, chess puzzles are such a specific genre precisely because real chess problems are very seldom of this sort. Ordinarily, much more general, varied, and open-ended strategies are called into play. To understand a real game is to explore the advantages and disadvantages of particular strategies in particular situations, viewing the end results in particular games not as definitive but simply as guides by which to generate new experiments in similar situations in the future. Indeed, chess genius involves precisely the ability to creatively transform old patterns whose possibilities everyone thought were exhausted.

In fact, then, even in a highly simplified context like chess games, problems emerge more as multidimensional problematic situations than as puzzles. That the real problems of life should somehow remain puzzles seems increasingly improbable. We might instead begin to wonder whether puzzles are not the special cases, those rare occasions when definitive and all-encompassing solutions really are possible. Maybe their relative rarity is why we need to invent artificial ones, to give ourselves the pleasure of decisively resolving something for once. But then the danger is that we will mistake the real problems of our lives for only another kind of puzzle.

This, at any rate, is the working hypothesis of a pragmatic style in ethics: that the multiplicity of values involved in ethical problems is essential, not merely a confusion that must be cleared away to reveal one or a few determinative issues. Ethical problems are typically the larger and vaguer regions of tension that define problematic situations. From a puzzle-solving point of view, of course, insisting on the essential complexity of a problem may look like a simple confession of failure, failure to find the key that will reveal the crucial underlying dimension or dimensions that make "solution" possible. At stake with pragmatism, correspondingly, is a shift in the very perception of complexity. Dewey calls for an understanding, acceptance, even celebration of complexity as deeply constitutive of our selves and our values. According to pragmatism, as defended here, it is essential to ethical problems that they have manifold dimensions, imperfectly integrated and seldom if ever reducible to one or a few determinative dimensions. Let us now ask what can be done with them.

Reconstructive Strategies

Toward Better Problems

When trying to solve a puzzle, challenging the constraints of the puzzle itself is ruled out from the start. Someone who "solves" crossword puzzles by changing the grid or rewriting the clues simply does not understand what a puzzle is. In problematic situations, however, the very shape of "the" problem itself may need to be rethought. We might almost say that someone who does *not* rethink "the" given problem itself does not understand what a problematic situation is. The very fact that dilemmas seem to arise only at certain points, for example, or are framed only as "episodes," may itself emerge as problematic. In addition, there may be better responses than the seemingly given options, and ultimately we may be able to change the very situation itself so that today's pressing problems arise in more tractable forms, or do not arise at all, in the future.

Looking at euthanasia in this light, for instance, once again yields a strikingly different set of questions from those usually raised. Remember V, the euthanasia candidate just introduced. Suppose that we ask why it is that V has landed in the Intensive Care Unit in the first place. What caused her accident, for instance? Badly maintained streets? Why are cars, in general, still so unsafe? And why has euthanasia, in general, become such a contentious issue?

Take just the last question. V is of course in a hospital, where more than 80 percent of all Americans now die. But in hospitals the actual point of death is increasingly not only a decision, as opposed to an event outside anyone's control, but is also a decision made by strangers. When those strangers are doctors, moreover, another compelling dimension of value is introduced. Deliberately standing by, doing nothing, while someone dies, may be emotionally unbearable. All of a doctor's training revolts against it. In short, an entire set of medical habits and practices almost guarantee that dying patients will be pitted against medical institutions in the ways we are now seeing, and that legal or quasi-legal rules will be necessary to settle matters.

In this way we can begin to bring into focus the larger problematic situation of which the puzzle about V is only one manifestation. Moreover, and crucially, these questions begin to suggest the possibility that the problematic situation itself might be changed, perhaps in the long run even eliminated. "The" problem of euthanasia seems to be posed by a very new way of dying. It is not a given but an entirely changeable social fact. Home care for the dying could be mandated, for example, at least as an option, and once doctors are off their own turf, and the hospital and its legal concerns are out of the picture, the balance of power may begin to shift back to patients and their families. Hospices, for another example, are designed to offer ameliorative medical care without necessarily prolonging a dying person's life. At present hospices are struggling along against medical opposition and governmental neglect, but there is no reason that this could not change.

This way of re-viewing "the" question of euthanasia also changes what we want to say even about immediate problems such as the case of V. In the first place, we become more able to acknowledge that there may be *no* self-sufficient or "final" answer to such problems considered by themselves, out of context. The specific problem of V may have no "solution" at all. Correspondingly, however, a wide range of partial and temporary responses becomes more plausible. Recognizing that all responses will necessarily be imperfect makes admittedly imperfect responses easier to accept.

Notice how the range of options in the case of V may change. We might come to accept quite a wide range of responses, so long as they are coupled with attempts, within our various limits, to change the larger problematic situation as well. V's doctors could propose keeping her alive until her family has recovered from the initial shock and can accept her death without feeling rushed into a decision. At the same time, doctors in such situations could begin to propose ways in which such decisions can be shifted back to patients and their families rather than being made by doctors and administrators. Hospices and home care, again, emerge as options. Doctors and administrators, along with the public and public officials, could actively promote both. Thus the focus of ethical attention begins to shift, and the demand for a decisive "solution" begins to be replaced by an exploration of more intelligent strategies to deal with the larger problem.

A great many suggestions along these lines are made in the pages to follow. In taking up the abortion issues in Chapter 3, for example, I eventually suggest that the most promising approach is one that systematically addresses the causes of unwanted pregnancy in the first place (e.g., lack of knowledge of and access to contraceptives, and the many forms of sexual coercion) and the social conditions that cast "the" issue itself in its present form (e.g., the medical control of abortion, social roles and career expectations still so rigid that an unplanned child can become an albatross around a woman's neck, and the disempowerment of women generally). The options that emerge with respect to "the" problem as it currently presents itself are correspondingly broadened and redirected. It is not somehow the end of the matter: perhaps hardly even the beginning.

"Preventive Ethics"

Ethical reconstruction in this sense is certainly not an invention of Dewey's. In a sense it is only an example of a kind of problem-solving technique that psychologists call "lateral thinking": making a kind of end run around what seems to be the immediate problem, still in the interests of resolving the underlying difficulty, although in a perhaps unexpected way. Correspondingly, being exclusively preoccupied with given problems and familiar kinds of solutions has been labeled "vertical thinking" or even "temporary functional blindness."[8]

As a very simple illustration, take the following situation. Some old friends of mine lived in a house so designed that when they wanted to use the fireplace they had to haul the wood through virtually the entire house to get it there. The result was that they seldom built fires, and when they did they made a huge mess. For years they just tried to carry wood more carefully. Later they were quite proud of themselves for hauling wood in a box, to avoid dropping splinters and dirt everywhere along the route. But this too was awkward. The halls were still small, the wood still large. Again they felt stuck. It took a precocious cousin to suggest that they simply knock a hole in the wall next to the fireplace and put in a small door and woodbin. My friends, in short, had become "blind" to an obvious and simple alternative because they were still preoccupied with better ways to haul wood through the house. In fact, the background causes and conditions that posed this problem—the design of the house itself—first had to be brought into focus and then had to be changed. The house itself needed "reconstruction." Notice then that the old problem—How can we haul wood through the house in a way that is not awkward and does not make a mess?—was not "solved" but rather circumvented, simply eliminated. It needs no answer.

Surely it is at least possible that the familiar ethical problems represent in part the dead ends of what we could call "vertical thinking" *in ethics*. In ethics too there may be the equivalent of houses so badly designed that we can only use them awkwardly, banging the ethical equivalent of the walls and littering the ethical equivalent of the floors. In ethics too, then, lateral thinking ought to be possible, making end runs around the familiar problems, changing the structures and background conditions within which they are posed, knocking a hole in the wall rather than devising ever more clever accommodations to the house as it is. If "the" problem of euthanasia can be largely prevented by a shift to hospice care for the dying, for example, or transformed by reempowering patients and their families, then the insistence that ethics must just address "the" question as it is currently posed—What should doctors do about seemingly hopeless cases, especially people they do not know at all, in the hospital?—is indeed another kind of vertical thinking. V's doctors do need some guidance, of course, but there is no reason to stop there—and again, as I have suggested, even the guidance we offer will be changed by the recognition of reconstructive options.

Above I suggested that we are often preoccupied with episodes, emergencies, and crisis thinking. This too is a kind of functional blindness. It leads to a failure to address the *causes* of those crises and emergencies. Irving Kenneth Zola analogizes the American medical system as a whole to a lifeguard so busy pulling drowning people out of the water that she can never ask why so many people are drowning in the first place. Medicine comes into play only after people are sick. Zola wants us to "refocus upstream," to think preventively, to improve nutrition and working conditions and water quality, so that desperate illness is less likely to arise in the first place.[9] Rather than devoting themselves to the ethical quandaries raised by lifeguarding, lateral thinkers would do better to leave the lifeguard to her last-ditch labors and march upstream to check the guardrails. Likewise, bioethics should take it upon itself to argue for more preventive measures, again, so that deciding the difficult and desperate cases finally just becomes much less necessary.[10]

Virginia Warren proposes a useful distinction between "crisis issues"—what I have called "episodes"—and "housekeeping issues," for which, as she puts it, "the problematic situation is ongoing, rather than resolved once and for all."[11] Keeping the guardrails maintained so that people do not fall into the river is an example of a housekeeping issue; saving them once they're drowning is a crisis issue. Daily mindfulness to one's loved ones is a housekeeping issue; going to a therapist to try to save a marriage on the rocks is a crisis issue. Crises do arise, of course, and sometimes overshadow everything else. But in a crisis we can still only jury-rig a partial response, usually within our lives and institutions as they are, including the very ways of life or institutions that create or perpetuate the problem. Emergency attention to crisis issues must be complemented by sustained attention to the background conditions that lead to crises, and by an attempt to address those conditions in such a way that crises are headed off. In a wonderful phrase, Warren calls this kind of ethics "preventive ethics," by analogy with preventive medicine. The ultimate task of medicine is not so much to cure disease as to prevent it; why might not the ultimate task of ethics be to *avert* the usual puzzles rather than to (try to) solve them? Or rather, why mightn't we *make* ethics that sort of enterprise?

Housekeeping issues are not exactly identical with the reconstructive questions I have tried to open. Reconstruction may be more radical and thoroughgoing. Getting truly informed and thoughtful consent, for example, is a housekeeping issue; reducing the need for obtaining such proxies in the first place is a reconstructive strategy. The term "preventive ethics" comes closer, I think, to the essential impulse of reconstructive strategies, but the overtones of "preventive" are more negative. "Refocussing upstream," meanwhile, captures *one* strategy for preventive thinking, but not the only one. What all of these terms serve to bring into focus, at any rate, are attempts to recast "the" problems we are currently given, to rethink their causes and conditions, and to ask whether there are not other kinds of resolutions to the larger problematic situation such that "the" immediate question, now seemingly so pressing, may not even arise at all. That is the essence of reconstruction's lateral thinking or end runs.

Warren does not claim that preventive or housekeeping issues should replace crisis issues in ethics—any more than preventive medicine can realistically replace crisis medicine—but only that crisis issues are very far from the whole story. Likewise, I do not want to say that reconstruction is the only strategy that ethics can use. Sometimes the given ethical questions can (or anyway must) in fact be answered, either in the traditional way or in some other way. In the next section I suggest an approach to answering them. The point here is just that reconstruction is at least *a* way of addressing them too. Deweyan ethics is sometimes not even recognized as an ethics, or else is regarded as a kind of evasion, precisely because its mode of engagement is so emphatically reconstructive. But I have argued that there is no reason to take "the" problems of ethics to be simply and solely the familiar episodic and crisis issues. Beyond, behind, and around them lie other issues and possibilities that may be far more promising for a genuinely ethical engagement.

Integrative Strategies

Values unavoidably come into tension, even if they do not exactly "conflict." Those tensions may well define problematic situations that press upon us in such a way that long-run reconstruction is not possible, or at any rate is not the only form of ethical engagement that we require. We must still act now. Thus a second kind of pragmatic method is necessary as well.

A nurse may believe that she owes all of her patients the same high level of care, perhaps on the grounds that such a nondiscriminating altruism is part of medicine's code of honor. But she may also believe that caring for others must be circumscribed by self-preservation and her obligations closer to home. Both views can easily be stated as ethical principles, and both principles have fine pedigrees. For that very reason, however, she will probably feel guilty charting the middle way that most of us would nonetheless be tempted to follow if the two principles conflict: offering "dangerous" patients somewhat more care and contact than we might consider really safe, but less than we might feel we "ought" to offer or might offer to others less threatening to ourselves. We are likely to satisfy neither principle, in short, though (and because) we are trying to honor the impulses behind both. And no third principle really fits this middle way. Instead we feel confused, and think ourselves morally weak.

Here the pragmatic impulse is to integrate, interweave, and combine values, seeing the "conflict" of values as an occasion to work out better forms of coexistence rather than to elevate one set of values over another. "Only dogmatism," says Dewey, "can suppose that serious moral conflict is between something clearly bad and something known to be good, and that uncertainty lies wholly in the will of the one choosing. Most conflicts of importance are conflicts between things which are or have been satisfying, not between good and evil."[12]

So it is in this case. The nurse's task is not to pick one direction or principle over the other. Both of her chief concerns matter. The challenge is to draw connections, to tease out the patterns and the relationships between her values, so that some coherent direction emerges in the particular case and some coherence emerges among her values looked at more broadly. "Choice," Dewey says, "is not the emergence of preference out of indifference. It is the emergence of a unified preference out of competing preferences." When such a preference does emerge,

> biases that had held one another in check now, temporarily at least, reinforce one another, and constitute a unified attitude. . . . Hence there is reasonable and unreasonable choice. . . . [In reasonable choice] the object thought of may be one which . . . unifies [and] harmonizes different competing tendencies. It may release an activity in which all are fulfilled, not indeed in their original form, but in a . . . way which modifies the original direction of each by [making] it a component along with others in an action of transformed quality.[13]

The nurse is asked, then, to begin to sort out the values at stake with the aim of *relating* them to each other, to her own and others' experience, to her sense of herself as a professional as well (perhaps) as a parent or spouse, and in any case as an individual with projects and hopes and fears beyond her professional identity. The task is to chart a course that honors and connects all of these values as well as she can. In this case at least, and for now, it may well be a middle way. Still, what is most compelling about it is not simply that it lies in the middle—for of course it might not; she might instead end up "unifying preference" in some other direction, a direction unsuspected when she first took up the question—but instead that it does indeed represent an "intelligently unified preference." A greater harmony arises out of disharmony; the competing values are fitted into a larger picture that hangs together as a whole and points the way to action.[14]

Commentary

That we tend toward "middle ways" in such situations is not surprising. Again, however, we are likely to feel that this tendency is a moral weakness. It is likely to lead to confusion and guilt. To the extent that we expect ethical problems to be puzzles, we will blame ourselves for failing to find simple and unequivocal answers.

Looked at from a pragmatic point of view, however, we should take pride in being able to find a middle way. For pragmatism, this kind of flexibility and accommodation is not a sign of weakness but is instead a sign of a mature sense of balance. What Dewey calls "modif[ying] the original direction of each [value] by [making] it a component along with others in an action of transformed quality" shows an appropriate sensitivity to circumstance and to the multiple values at stake in the situation.

Still, the proposal is not simply that the nurse *compromise* between the different values in this situation. Compromise is more like a last resort. The integrative impulse goes deeper. It attempts to *harmonize* values, to weave conflicting and diverse values into a pattern or story (we shall see that many different forms are possible) that gives us a way to relate them, to connect them, to try to make sense of them together, allowing them to differ without making the tension totally intractable. The nurse might for example come to see herself as a caring person trying to respond to the different needs of others with appropriately different kinds of care, keeping in mind her own needs as well.[15]

"Well then," someone might say, "why not 'harmonize' values under an ethical principle or theory? That too would reduce them to consistency, clearing the way for action." But the very language of this proposal—"reduce to consistency," "clear the way"—betrays its real spirit. It rests upon a refusal to acknowledge that the relevant values might be too rich and too varied to fit under one or a few general rules. It does not "weave" them together. Contemporary ethical philosophers might regard the "integration" proposed here as a kind of lesser evil. If values really turn out to conflict irremediably, then some sort of cobbled-together, low-level principle (so the middle way may seem to them) will at least be better than nothing. But this is to treat the very richness and diversity of values as an exception, even as a kind of defeat, whereas for Dewey it is the norm, and not at all a defeat but instead a kind of opportunity. Acknowledge our values in their diversity and conflict, and the challenge becomes not one of reducing them, but of interlinking them in a way that does not deny their difference while still weaving them together into a coherent and livable pattern. The challenge is not so much to clear a way as to *find* a way.

Some choices do seem to be all or nothing. A pregnant woman must either carry the child or choose abortion. Jean-Paul Sartre's young student during World War II must either stay with his mother in occupied Paris or go off to England to join the Free French. But it certainly does not follow, from the fact that *actions* must (sometimes) be all or nothing in this way, that our *ethical reasoning* must also be so simplified. Even though our actions must sometimes fall on one side or the other of a radical dichotomy, it certainly does not follow that decision making must be equally dichotomous. Nonethical choices, like deciding to move or buying a car, may also be all or nothing. Ultimately you must either move or not. But rare is the person who thinks that she must decide such matters "on principle" or who blames herself for taking her time or looking for middle ways.

Moreover, the most important point to notice about such cases is how readily we presume that our choices must be all or nothing rather than recognizing even the most basic psychological complexities of such cases and making use of (or, God forbid, even expanding) the "room for play" that they open up. A nurse, for example, has an enormous range of possible ways of treating any individual person available to her. She can treat minimally and professionally, she can give of herself in a variety of ways, she can take special precautions in a variety of ways, and so on. To imagine that the choice is somehow simply yes or no is to wildly oversimplify the situation.

Sartre's young man is an even more surprising case, since although this example has been very widely discussed, almost no one has noticed that the young man has far more creative options than the two he poses for himself. Why couldn't he stay with his mother long enough to wean her from her (alleged) dependence, for instance, and *then* head for England? Or why couldn't he work for the Free French *in* Paris—spying, or sabotaging? Dangerous work, to be sure, but so is heading across occupied country to England to fight on the front lines. And even this is still only the crudest and most obvious level on which to work. Any good counselor would ask much more. Must the situation itself be accepted as absolutely given? Is the father intractable? Is the mother really so graspingly dependent or is she perhaps capable of a little patriotism and independence too? And has the son even asked her what she wants? Again, both Sartre and the young man himself seem far too ready to assume the fixity of the situation.

Dewey and other pragmatists also stress the fluidity of values themselves, especially in situations of uncertainty.[16] Consider again Sartre's poor young man. Surely Sartre is wrong to treat the young man's values as fixed. The young man might for example rethink his somewhat hotheaded attraction to violence. Would his murdered brother (one factor that weighs on both him and his mother, in different ways) insist on retribution at such cost? Might the young man even implicitly be asking Sartre to help him rethink what he actually owes to his mother, especially if, as sounds possible, she is using the specter of her own helplessness to manipulate his feelings? The young man's situation, while shaped by a number of deeply held values (Sartre is wrong about that too; if the young man's values were really arbitrary, as Sartre claims, his choice would not be anguishing), is in fact ambiguous and complex, and for that very reason allows more options than the two radically opposed choices with which he begins. Ethical thinking ought to move him *beyond* an insistence on all-or-nothing choices and all-or-nothing principles.[17]

Toward a "Holistic" Ethical Method

Integrating values is no mystery, any more than reconstructing values is a mystery. We are already entirely capable of integrating values when the question at hand is not classified as ethical: when it is a question of choosing a house or changing jobs or rethinking a relationship. Here too an entire range of factors is involved, and finding a livable balance may be immensely difficult. Here too an extensive psychological literature has grown up to help. These problems may be just as difficult, or even more difficult, than those we usually think of as ethical. But here it occurs to us *not* to try to integrate the values at stake, let alone to feel guilty for doing so.

Here too we are also very cautious about speaking of "right" and "wrong" choices, at least until much later, after we have seen how things work out. At the time we may speak of more or less intelligent or creative strategies, well-considered choices, ways of carrying on that most effectively invoke what we might call the "center of gravity" of our values: the basic thrust of the best integration of our values that we can manage at the time. Sometimes, indeed, we may wish to speak only of ways of carrying on that give our values a more definite direction, a more definite center of gravity, than they have had so far, perhaps even just as a kind of experiment. Only in ethics does it seem that these skills, and this flexibility and caution, are disengaged.

Still, like some reconstructive strategies, some of these integrative skills are being reinvoked, at least in partial ways, in contemporary ethics. As we shall see in Chapter 6, for example, John Rawls's method of "reflective equilibrium" is in fact an integrative method, though I will argue that it must be kept distinct from some other more abstract and traditional features of Rawls's approach. Rawls argues that a number of different values must be balanced together, along with the results of certain thought-experiments, in formulating principles of justice. Harmonizing values into a single coherent account is crucial; I will only argue that it needn't be restricted to the level of principles or theories.[18]

Or again, Carol Gilligan's well-known work *In a Different Voice* contrasts the supposedly impersonal and absolute dictates of justice with an approach based on "care," which requires us to weigh and balance a wide range of different commitments and concerns in order to decide what to do. For Gilligan, central to the ethical orientations of at least some people is a strong sense of relationship: of overlapping and binding linkages of dependence, care, and love for specific other people. But nothing guarantees that all of the different demands involved will be consistent. Thus once again we are faced with a number of different values that must be balanced together, teased into a workable way forward. The integrative approach proposed here, however, goes beyond the integration of care values. *All* values arise in linkages of these sorts.[19]

In their recent and widely read defense of casuistry, Albert Jonsen and Stephen Toulmin begin by contrasting two senses of the word "argument": "Theoretical arguments are chains of proofs, whereas practical arguments are methods for resolving problems. In the first, formal sense, an argument is a 'chain' of propositions, linked up so as to guarantee its conclusion. In the second, substantive sense, an argument is a network of considerations, presented so as to resolve a practical quandary."[20] Jonsen and Toulmin argue for "arguments" in the second sense, a project they identify with casuistical patterns of moral thinking, patterns well developed during medieval times and unjustly maligned, in their view, since then. Not all casuistical thinking as they characterize it is very integrative—analogical reasoning is not necessarily integrative, for example—but the notion of constructing "networks of values" surely is. Again a kind of careful weaving-together is called for. Jonsen and Toulmin also stress the flexibility and open-endedness of casuistical thinking, and its sensitivity to the particulars of specific cases. One locates oneself not with respect to a fixed body of principles that determine practice when properly applied, but instead within a large and evolving set of prior judgments and provisional rules that do not so much determine a single right answer as lay out a range of more or less acceptable possibilities.[21]

So times are changing. But integrative methods still cause profound disquiet among some philosophers. Some philosophers can see only anarchy and "relativism" beyond the traditional "moral geometry" that pragmatists as well as all of the writers just cited reject. Some even claim that integrative approaches miss the point of ethics itself, since there is a way in which integrative approaches seem (*seem*) to preclude taking a critical stance toward values themselves. Other philosophers believe that decisions are not possible at all without some appeal beyond the networks of values of which we have been speaking. To arbitrate between two competing values, it is argued, we must have recourse to some other value or values held as standards and not at stake in the arbitration itself. Consequently, the argument concludes, to arbitrate among our values in general we must have recourse to some general value or values, again held as standards and not themselves at stake, apparently, in *any* arbitration about values.[22] Ethical thinking is simply impossible without some kind of fixed principles.

At the end of this book I will briefly take up the objections about relativism and the possibility of criticism. The last argument, however, fundamentally misunderstands holistic thinking itself and must be briefly addressed here.

It does not follow that because we arbitrate between specific values by reference to other values held constant for the moment, some values must always be held constant. The "reference" for specific arbitrations will always be the "center of gravity" of our values generally: the general thrust of the best integration that we can manage at any given time. But with enough shifting of specific values, this center of gravity itself may shift. No external standard is necessary.

This is perfectly obvious in nonethical cases. I don't decide what career to pursue by reference to some external standard. Instead I work within my own values, trying to bring out their central tendencies, recognizing also that my eventual choices may well change some of those very tendencies in the long run. In psychology, the "theory of cognitive dissonance" has been describing such processes for decades.[23] Philosophical "holists" describe the process of trying to reweave our beliefs and values into larger and more coherent sets. Otto Neurath's familiar analogy about rebuilding a ship at sea addresses this very point. A ship can be entirely rebuilt at sea, staying afloat all the while.

Integrative thinking, then, is not at all unheard of, either theoretically or practically. It goes on constantly all around us. Indeed it is astonishing that the way of thinking so routinely employed with respect to nearly all of our values should be thought not just unwise but somehow impossible when it comes to ethical values. Philosophical ethics seems to have strayed from practical thinking about values.[24] What remains, at any rate, is to insist upon integrative and reconstructive thinking as a coherent and sustained kind of ethical practice after all. And the best way to do so, as I have already promised, is in practice.

Chapter 3

Rethinking the Abortion Debate

ABORTION may not be the most fortunate of ethical problems to take up at the start. We might do better to turn first to general questions of lifestyle or social welfare or the human relation to nature. Even with respect to abortion "the" issue may be far broader than it usually seems, which perhaps is why it has stayed alive so long. But we will come to these other questions in time. Now, however, abortion is one of the most salient problems that confronts us. If it is an unfortunate place-holder for so central a place, that too is part of the problem.

Against Drawing Lines

Much of the rhetoric of the popular abortion debate centers around the question whether fetuses are or are not "human." It is assumed that if fetuses are human, then they have the same moral weight as the rest of us, and that if they aren't, then they don't.

But "human" proves to be an ambiguous category, which has made for a lot of bad arguments. Human fetuses are obviously *human* fetuses ("What else could they be?" as the popular argument goes). They have distinctively human chromosomes, human growth patterns, and so on. But the same could be said of any part of the human body. Even our hair and our saliva contain distinctively human genetic material. Two senses of the word "human" seem to be run together here. In one sense, "human" just names a genetic category. In the other sense, it names a kind of being: human being, a certain sort of whole creature with certain distinctive capacities. Fetuses are obviously human, then, but whether they are human *beings* is not so clear.

The category "human" is also misleading in another way. Non-human creatures might also have the relevant wholeness and the relevant capacities for having what we tendentiously call "human" rights. Suppose that whales, or great apes, or some variety of extraterrestrial, turn out to think and feel in the relevant ways very much as we do. According to the usual argument, they would be candidates, at least, for having rights—not by virtue of being human, however, but simply by virtue of being creatures with the sorts of self-consciousness and needs that ground rights. Maybe only humans in fact have such capacities and therefore rights; maybe other creatures do too. In any case the question cannot be answered by mere fiat or by the unsurprising accident that the rights-holders we happen to know best are ourselves.[1]

The usual conclusion is that we need a category other than "human" or "human being" to designate the set of beings who have the special character, and consequently the serious ethical weight, that we attribute to ourselves. Philosophers have adopted the word "person" for this purpose. Adult, normally conscious humans are taken to be unproblematically persons. Maybe certain extraterrestrials, or some other animals, are persons too. And the question about fetuses can then be put very precisely. Are fetuses persons? Do they have the sorts of rights that we call "human" rights, the sort of ethical weight that "we" have?

Drawing a Line

Of course, the answer is not at all clear. Some philosophers define "person" so restrictively that not even all humans count; others define it so broadly that many other animals count too.

Many proposed definitions center around having a concept of self and the capacity to project a future. Michael Tooley, for example, argues that only creatures who have a sense of self and can project a future can have desires about themselves and about their futures, and that only creatures with such desires can be said to have rights against their frustation. But Tooley's argument is also highly controversial. In the end it becomes an argument not only for legalizing abortion but also for legalizing some forms of infanticide.[2]

A more common strategy avoids defining "person" directly and instead argues for the *continuity* of fetuses with human persons after birth. Many opponents of abortion ("conservatives," in the usual philosophical terminology) therefore hold that there is no point in fetal development that marks a radical enough change to justify attributing personhood after the change but denying it before the change. Not even birth, they say, makes *that* kind of difference. The fetus does become independent of its mother's body at birth, for instance, but dependent beings can still be persons. Newborns are hardly less dependent on constant care. Late-term fetuses, moreover, are capable of living outside the womb. They are, in medical terms, "viable." The onset of viability itself is sometimes taken as another possible place to "draw the line," but for the conservative, viability does not mark a radical enough change either. As medical technology advances, moreover, the point of viability shifts earlier and earlier and becomes progressively less definite.

According to the conservative argument, then, we must look earlier and earlier for a place to draw the line. But at each step the argument stresses continuity, the gradualness of the changes involved. At each step we find ourselves unable to deny the child or fetus personhood at a single stroke. Finally, via this "slippery slope," we arrive at the very beginning. Conception is the only possible line.[3]

"Liberal" views are more varied, but nearly all "draw a line" somewhere, though not always as late as birth. The underlying argument is often just the conservatives' argument stood on its head. Where a conservative would have us imagine a child and then slowly trace back that child's development, stressing continuity all the way back to conception, a liberal may have us begin by imagining the just-fertilized egg and then trace fetal development *forward*, stressing continuity all the way to birth. Clearly, the argument begins, the just-fertilized egg is not a person. How could this little bit of matter, just two or four cells, be the moral equivalent of one of us? But since development after conception is gradual, we once again find ourselves unable to attribute the fetus personhood at a single stroke. Now we must look later and later in search of a place to draw the line. Finally we arrive at the very end: birth (or, sometimes, viability) is the only possible line. We are again on a slippery slope, in short, only now it is sloping in the other direction. It is not so much a slope as a teeter-totter.[4]

Even the extremes of fetal development are not necessarily extreme enough for this logic. Conservatives argue against liberals that even birth does not mark a radical enough change to make the difference between persons and nonpersons. If so, then liberals have no way at all to draw a line, or they must draw it still later, like Tooley, thus seeming to allow some kinds of infanticide. But likewise some liberals argue that we cannot draw a radical line at conception. As Joel Feinberg puts it,

> why grant the right to life to the zygote but not to the ovum or spermatozoon, which are also, in some intelligible sense, "potential human beings"[?] The zygote, of course, has the *full* genetic complement of a specific potential human being, but that shows simply that the zygote's human potentiality is more proximate than the spermatozoon's, actualizable in less time with fewer combinatorial processes, and more likely in fact to eventuate— big differences, no doubt, but differences in degree for all that.[5]

Notice: "differences in degree for all that." Again the claim is that the difference in question is not a radical enough difference to mark the attainment of personhood itself. But the required change must be radical indeed if not even conception or birth could count. What *could* count?

Why Draw a Line?

I do not propose to draw a line in some new or hitherto over-looked place. Pragmatism asks something very different from us. I have suggested that a pragmatic outlook is not concerned with "moral geometry" in the sense that pragmatism's aim is not to deduce the solutions to well-defined puzzles from moral first principles. Pragmatism is also, partly as a consequence, much less concerned with the literal "moral geometry" of drawing lines that mark radical differences in moral status. If the familiar yes-or-no questions are so hard to answer with respect to the fetus, why should we assume that we have here a particularly difficult puzzle rather than something that is not a puzzle at all? Why, in short, draw lines at all? Why suppose that personhood must be acquired at a single stroke?

Remember that the alleged necessity of drawing a line gets no support from the actual facts of fetal development. In fact, as I have just been suggesting, what is startling about the familiar conservative and liberal arguments is that it is the very gradualness of fetal development that they insist upon, however little they really honor it. The demand to draw a line must come from elsewhere. Again we must ask: If no single change in that long process of radical transformation seems quite radical enough to alone mark the difference between personhood and nonpersonhood, why should we nonetheless insist that one single change must mark that difference in the first place? Why one line? Why *any* lines?

For some philosophical and religious traditions, personhood is marked by having a soul, and since the soul is by nature unitary and nonmaterial, it follows that "ensoulment" must be both a single event and a radical, qualitative transformation. I shall assume that this reason to draw a line will not tempt many readers of this volume. But remembering this context does perhaps raise the pitch of the question still further. Without a notion of ensoulment, would we even have been tempted to believe that personhood arrives suddenly? Why should becoming a person be any different from becoming an adult, or an alcoholic, or a good swimmer: something that is gradual and even agonizingly slow?

I suspect that the main reasons are to be found in certain epistemological habits. It is very tempting to suppose that the denotation of a concept is like a territory that one enters at a definite instant.[6] It follows that there must be some definite point at which any concept, personhood included, first applies to any given thing. Meanwhile too, the venerable Principle of the Excluded Middle holds that, for every thing and every property, either the thing has that property or it (simply) doesn't. It follows that the fetus either is a person or it (simply) isn't. Maybe it is hard to tell which, but there is still supposed to be a fact of the matter. Ambiguity does not go all the way down.

Whatever the reason, in any case, the alleged necessity of drawing a line is never systematically defended, as far as I know, and is hardly ever even raised as a question, in the massive literature (philosophical and other) on abortion. But the question must be raised. Even the strict philosophical arguments are far from persuasive. For one thing, the existence of gradual transformations is a *problem* for the Principle of the Excluded Middle. After a while a constant flow of sand produces a heap, grain by grain, but it is not at all clear that it must become a heap at some one single instant in that process. Similar is the problem of "vague predicates," such as color terms. A color that lies in the middle range between red and orange is neither red nor not-red. It is not exactly red, because of course there is a difference between it and a clear shade of red. But it is not therefore not-red either, because there is still an important similarity between it and clear shades of red. Room must be opened for concepts without classically sharp boundaries.

Or again, we seem to apply certain concepts by comparing putative instances with paradigm cases or "templates," in which case infinite degrees of similarity and dissimilarity with the paradigm case are absolutely to be expected. Other concepts appear to be "cluster concepts," groupings any pair of whose instances share certain features, but not necessarily the same ones. Here the boundaries are unclear both because what exactly qualifies even the uncontested cases is not easy to pin down, and because there will presumably be a number of cases that possess many, but perhaps not quite enough, of the relevant features. Family resemblances fade out slowly. Even second cousins may have that inimitable Smith smile.[7]

What then of persons? "Person" seems, in the first place, to be a cover term for a large and varied set of features, not all of which need be present, and no one of which may be decisive, in any given case. "Person," in short, is a good candidate for a cluster concept. Persons tend to perceive, speak a language, use tools; to have a concept of self, generalize and draw conclusions from past experience, see themselves as one such self among others; to project a future, have desires about it, and know their own mortality; to joke, be angry, doubt, love, work with others; to be descended of other persons; to be sexed; to have the ability to own property, to be legally liable in certain contexts; and so on. No doubt more features can be added. But none of these features may be an absolutely necessary condition for being a person. "Person" may be a concept without a core. It seems more likely that, as Jane English puts it, "there are only features which are more or less typical."[8]

Moreover, even if these "typical" features were individually acquired at a single stroke, personhood itself would still be developed in a gradual way. Personhood is a matter of a certain variable constellation of features, not of just one or two. Certain clusters of these features clearly make for persons, then, while the same clusters with a few features not yet developed are incipient persons, not yet persons but far closer to personhood than to nonpersonhood. Still less developed are, say, fetuses at seven months, farther from personhood but emphatically not just elaborate pieces of tissue. Finally, many of the farther features of personhood are themselves acquired gradually: language, love, even our characteristic individual shapes. Thus we have not so much even a "slope" as a kind of summation of many slopes. Becoming a person is a long and bumpy ride.

Gradualism

Personhood, then, is *not* all or nothing. A being can become a person gradually. Indeed, as far as we know, the gradual way is the only way possible. At conception the conceptus has virtually none of the features that make for human persons. A newborn has many, though by no means all or even most of them. In between, more are gradually developed. Also developing gradually are a number of other characteristics, such as the capacity to feel pain, a recognizably human form, and so on, not all of them directly tied to personhood. What we need in general is not a single sharp line but a set of careful descriptions of just what features fetuses (and, when necessary, other incipient persons) have at what times. These descriptions will of course be complicated, and many of the necessary details are not yet even known.

Such a developmental view of the fetus dramatically changes the complexion of the abortion question. It is no longer a matter of either insisting that the fetus *is* (unqualifiedly) a person, and so has exactly the moral weight that you or I have, or that the fetus is *not* a person (at all), and so has no moral weight at all. In fact fetuses are neither persons nor nonpersons, but something in between, and furthermore are constantly changing. Acknowledging this intermediate and changing developmental status suggests a similarly intermediate and changing moral status. No justification remains for trying to draw sharp and absolute moral lines when there are no such lines in the actual phenomena. The moral weight we attach to fetuses because of their personlike characteristics must come in gradations.

I have accused the "conservative" and "liberal" positions on abortion of failing to take fetal development seriously. To do better we need a view that we might call "gradualism." Gradualism simply suggests that the strength of the fetus's moral claims steadily increases as it matures. Stronger and stronger countervailing reasons are required to justify abortion as the fetus develops. Near conception even fairly minor countervailing reasons are sufficient to override the claims of the conceptus or embryo. Later in pregnancy, by contrast, much stronger reasons are required to override the fetus's claims. Even late in pregnancy, many aspects of personhood are almost entirely lacking in the fetus, but others—most crucially, perhaps, a degree of consciousness—have developed. And these are grounds for *some* serious consideration.[9]

The logic of gradualism is not at all unfamiliar. All sorts of values wax and wane in gradual rather than sudden ways. Attachment and commitment, even to another person, grow slowly. There are no sharp lines. The more effort you put into your community or your home the harder it is to leave. After a time it becomes quite wrenching; after a further time, perhaps, impossible; but again there are no sharp lines. Once again this gradualism is entirely obvious and hardly worth mentioning when the values in question are not classified as ethical. It is time to recognize that ethical values are at the very least no less subtle.[10]

We return below to the question of how gradualism might work with respect to abortion decisions. This question, however, can be answered only in the context of an overall pragmatic approach to the abortion issue. To understand how and why someone might choose to leave a community or a home, for example, it is not enough to recognize that the values of a particular community or home grow on us slowly. We must also recognize what kinds of values impel us to move—and for that matter what *other* kinds of values impel us to stay. Thus with abortion: the picture is larger than the one we have so far drawn. It turns out that pragmatism's abandonment of the familiar "moral geometry" has a second and further dramatic consequence for the abortion debate, and it is this that we must take up first.

Multiple Relevant Values

Pragmatism's pluralism insists that no single value—personhood or any other—is the whole story. As in any other problematic situation, there are no automatically definitive values. We therefore must pay more careful attention—and less immediately judgmental attention—to the *other* values at stake in abortion decisions. Thus it is not merely that the personlike moral weight of the fetus comes in degrees. It is also that the moral ins and outs of abortion are by no means exhausted by the question of fetal personhood, even if approached in a gradualistic way. Gradualism only opens the door to the consideration of a much wider range of revelant values.

Even If the Fetus Is Not a Person

Even if the fetus is not a person, ending its existence quite probably causes it to suffer. Research increasingly suggests that fetal experience is complex and extensive; viewing the fetus as just a collection of cells, insensitive to anything that is done to it, is increasingly indefensible.[11] How much suffering abortion causes, and what kind, are among those difficult but still factual questions that need more research. Suffering may be rationalized by other sorts of benefits (indeed we seem to think nothing of imposing extraordinary suffering on some other creatures for benefits that are often quite dubious, a point to which Chapter 4 returns), but nonetheless, at the very least, it is a cost, a harm, that demands some kind of accounting.

Moreover, here the suffering is not merely inflicted on a being that nonetheless retains its integrity through the pain. The fetus is almost always destroyed. Abortion is unavoidably a violent act, and as such it is also a kind of violation, a fundamental rupturing of connection. The texture of both our individual lives and of the ethical community is changed when such violence becomes an acknowledged and regular practice among us. Many doctors, even those who are pro-choice, decline to perform abortions for this reason. It too must be taken seriously.

Then there is the vexing matter of the potential of the fetus. It is a vexing matter partly because even here the personhood model tends to distort the debate. Potential tends to be invoked as potential personhood, sometimes as almost-actual personhood.[12] But it seems more accurate to describe the felt loss not as something that is already, or will become, an individual with rights, but instead as the locus of a potential set of relationships and dependencies. What is at stake is the deepening and thickening of the web of relationships and love that a child promises. This deepening may begin even early in pregnancy. "There were changes happening in my body," says one woman in Carol Gilligan's abortion study, "and I felt very protective."[13] This is a precious thing. Again, it is not the end of the matter—in fact, this woman still chose abortion, a decision that her interviewer accepts—but it surely is precious all the same. Women who have experienced involuntary miscarriage speak of the same sense of loss. The loss is not just the barely developed creature that actually miscarries.

Related both to potential and to the larger question of humanness is the fact that fetuses soon develop recognizably human form. Accustomed to exalting mind over body, philosophers tend to discount form. Some psychological work, however, suggests that we should not be so sure. The human form in others invokes deepseated patterns of projection, identification, and sympathy. Mary Midgley, Leon Kass, and others have argued at length that such features are not morally irrelevant at all.[14]

This question too may be distorted by the apparatus of personhood. The general notion of personhood makes these emotional identifications and sympathies particularly hard to recognize and speak for. Appeals to form may seem to regress to identifying persons with humans, and appeals to sympathy may seem to replace the search for clear criteria with an emotional and intuitive sense of connection that does not lend itself easily to impersonal philosophical or legal arguments. But a pragmatic view can and ought to take these appeals more seriously. For one thing, the pragmatist is not attempting to characterize persons as such, but simply to characterize our particular connections to one class of beings, maybe or maybe not falling under the category "persons" but anyway having a definite character of their own. Felt connection, then, need not carry the entire weight, and therefore it becomes conceivable that it might at least carry *some*. And although impersonal arguments are no doubt necessary in some contexts, we might also consider that part of the very problem is that profoundly personal connections are at stake here. How they can be spoken for in impersonal contexts is not clear, but the answer is certainly not to deny that felt connection has any significance at all.

Again, none of this is surprising. Except when we are in the throes of the radically polarized contemporary debate, everyone recognizes that the abortion of a fetus represents a profound and disturbing loss—even if, again, it is sometimes the lesser evil. It surprises no one when women who have experienced involuntary miscarriages report a deep sense of loss. It may not even surprise us to discover that physicians can be prosecuted for murder if a fetus survives abortion and the doctor fails to make good-faith efforts to keep it alive.[15] Such are the paradoxes with which we live.

Even If the Fetus Is a Person

Meanwhile, the question is hardly closed even if the fetus is a person. In the first place, obviously, the fetus is not the only person involved. Oddly enough, this needs to be insisted upon. The personhood framework is often inconsistently applied in the abortion debate. The personhood of the fetus is emphasized, but the fact that fetuses are after all carried by persons, pregnant women, tends to be obscured. Many of the photographs of (live) fetuses so prominent in anti-abortion campaigns airbrush out the pregnant woman entirely, so that the fetus is literally floating in empty space. The pregnant woman vanishes into a black hole. But the fact is that fetuses are carried by women who are themselves persons—much less problematically than fetuses, too, one would think—with life projects and choices and energies that are profoundly and irreversibly affected by their pregnancies.

The rest of the argument only spells out the implications of this fact. The most fundamental acknowledgment of personhood is the right of self-determination. Correspondingly, it is the most fundamental kind of disempowerment to deny a woman the right to determine what happens to her own body, and therefore to profoundly restructure her life not only without her consent but often against her will. There is no other situation in which we even *consider* imposing so fundamentally upon a person's right to determine what happens with his or her own body. As Judith Thompson has argued, for example, we would not require any person unwillingly to donate his or her body parts or to allow his or her body to be tapped for life support, even if another person's life depended upon it.[16] There is no excuse for imposing such outcomes upon pregnant women.

Those who want to make fetal rights the end of the matter are inconsistent in another way also. If fetuses are indeed persons, they are hardly less persons if they are conceived as a result of rape. Yet most of the anti-abortion movement is willing to grant an exception in the case of pregnancy due to rape.[17] It appears that personhood is not the whole story after all, even for the anti-abortion movement. But then the alleged personhood of the fetus cannot be used as a conclusive argument in other cases. Could there not also be very profound threats to the integrity of a woman's self, or her autonomy, or even her life, in cases of pregnancy caused by, say, contraceptive failure? In short, if the personhood of the fetus is not sufficient to bar abortion when pregnancy is due to rape, why is it supposed to be sufficient otherwise?

One may answer that the personhood of the pregnant woman has been violated if she is pregnant due to rape, while her personhood has not been violated if the pregnancy is due to contraceptive failure. But this response misses the point. In the first place, it does not explain why abortion in case of rape becomes acceptable. The rape itself is now irremediable. How then—strictly in terms of personhood—could anything be rectified by aborting the "innocent fetus"? But the striking fact is, again, that most of us more or less agree, despite the depth and severity of closely related disagreements, that abortion is acceptable in the case of pregnancy due to rape. And to explain this agreement we must understand the problem in a way that finally undercuts the attempt to distinguish pregnancy due to rape from pregnancy due to other causes. It is not just personhood, at least as currently understood, that rape violates. A larger kind of integrity, less easily articulated, is at stake. One's body, most importantly, must be acknowledged as central to one's self, so that rape must be understood as violating not just a woman's autonomy or freedom of choice but her very self. Only (some?) men, perhaps, have the luxury of treating their bodies as inessential to "who they are." Once we acknowledge the body as central to the self, however, then *any* pregnancy, whether due to rape or not, must be recognized as affecting the very core of who one is.[18]

These less easily articulated values have been addressed by some writers—notably mostly by female writers, in contrast to the largely male-authored "rights" and personhood literature—in recent years. Some of these writers remind us that personhood, both as a real legal status and as an experience of one's self, is by no means secure for many women even now. Real concern for persons must therefore take seriously the problem of nurturing personhood, rather than simply assuming a woman's personhood in theory but then ignoring it in practice in favor of the much more problematic personhood of fetuses. Other writers focus on the ways in which care arises in the relation between mother and fetus, rather than from what are supposed to be completely independent characteristics of fetuses in themselves.[19]

Still other vital values are also at stake. The strain of a child, or of another child, may be too great on the relationships that ground and give meaning to a woman's life. Or a woman's own life projects, her own deepest hopes and aspirations for herself, may be too deeply imperiled. Both of these kinds of concern are absolutely basic, yet neither is truly an invocation of personhood. One's personhood on the popular philosophical view is never tied up with one's children or family, so considerations about the strain of another child, compelling as they may be, simply do not enter the picture so long as we think solely in terms of personhood. Yet these reasons—invoking a very literal kind of self-defense, and a defense of other people one loves—remain compelling reasons. They are the reasons that pregnant women again and again give for seeking abortion, even when abortion has been illegal and dangerous.[20]

One further consideration cuts across those so far introduced. This has to do with the quality of life of the potential child. One condition under which the case for abortion seems particularly strong is if the child otherwise would be born severely retarded or with fatal physical defects. Even some people on the anti-abortion side would allow such exceptions. Of course, it might be argued that a severely retarded fetus is not in fact a person in a full enough sense to have the rights normally associated with persons. But this is perilous territory for a movement that wants to insist on the personhood even of the conceptus, a microscopic being that cannot hold a candle to any fetus, no matter how "defective." If fetuses are persons, fetuses with severe physical defects surely are no less persons for having those afflictions.

It is better to recognize this exception, like the exception made for rape, for what it is: an acknowledgment that something besides personhood also carries ethical weight. A very short life, accompanied by immense suffering all around, may not be a good enough life to insist on saving, even if in some sense it is the life of a person. And even a long life, if accompanied by constant suffering and bereft of most of the opportunities that we usually feel make life worth living, may not be a good enough life to insist on saving. Inevitably, again, there are other values at stake beside personhood.

Deciding the Question: An Integrative Approach

Abortion decisions, then, are not puzzles. They arise from problematic situations. A variety of different values and types of values are in tension, some directly related and some only distantly or ambiguously connected to each other. There is no single definitive value or principle. It is not a matter of just putting on our puzzle-solving caps. It would be better to start at the opposite end, so to speak: with the recognition that there is no perfectly satisfactory answer. The choice may be tragic whatever one chooses. This is the way that some theologians, at least, have put the point.[21] So dense are the contending values here that there may be no way to proceed without doing violence to something that matters, and probably matters profoundly.

In a sense this is obvious. I do not offer it as a new discovery. Still, however, the temptation to reduce the abortion issue to a puzzle is widespread and apparently also natural.[22] Just complicating the issue, unfortunately, is a certain kind of progress. The argument of the previous sections, then, has not been a kind of prelude to pragmatic thinking, but part of pragmatic engagement itself. Recognizing problematic situations as such is the first step toward effectively addressing them.

Now, however, we must take the next step. We must begin to ask how pragmatism would suggest actually deciding what to do, given the problematic situation as so far characterized. This question itself has several levels.

Legal Gradualism

The assertion and defense of abortion as a legal right, whether one exercises the right or not, has dominated the public and philosophical discussion of abortion. I therefore want to begin by drawing some conclusions about the social regulation of abortion.

I have proposed in the first place to view the fetus's claims as developing gradually rather than suddenly. We do not confront a full-scale claim from the start, though we also cannot deny any claim at all until the end. Instead, gradually increasing claims on the part of the fetus need to be weighed alongside a wide range of other revelant claims and values. I have also argued that many of the other values at stake do not reduce to dimensions of personhood. The decision is not simply a matter of the relative priority of persons or of partial persons. Instead the "weighing" or "balancing" required is inevitably a broader and more open-ended project.

Taken together, these arguments make it impossible to continue to claim that one of the values at stake—"life," which in the current lingo actually means the life of the fetus—is so overwhelmingly important as to automatically override all of the other values at stake in all cases. Again, obviously, if in the early stages of development fetuses are not persons, we can no longer justify prohibiting abortion on the grounds that personhood is fully present and overridingly important from the start. Even at later stages of development, fetal life is not the automatically overriding value. Thus, choosing "life"—again, the life of the fetus—cannot be made mandatory for everyone.

We require a legal gradualism to match this moral gradualism, and it is from this vantage point that we can suggest that a framework like the Supreme Court's 1973 decision in *Roe v. Wade* is appropriate for public policy toward abortion. *Roe*, of course, drew not one line but three, dividing pregnancy by trimester and thus in effect codified a gradualist framework, setting higher and higher standards for abortion as the fetus matures. Admittedly the Court's legal argument could be tighter, but *Roe* is nonetheless a humane and appropriate decision from a pragmatic perspective. That the Court just say "yes" or "no," that abortion as such either be legalized or criminalized, is simply not an appropriate expectation.

This will seem to be a "pro-choice" view, at least as the current fault lines of the debate go. But I want to stress that we come to this view for structural sorts of reasons that arise out of the attempt in these pages to rethink the abortion debate as a whole. There is a vital asymmetry in the two popular positions. "Pro-choice" is not anti-"life"; the argument is only that other values also matter, that the appeal to "life" does not close the question. "Pro-life," however, *is* anti-"choice"; the claim is that the value of one of the lives in question overrides all other values and all other lives, and precludes any other choice. I have disputed this claim on structural grounds, as it were, rather than substantive grounds: not because some *other* value—"choice" itself, maybe, or pregnant women's rights—is automatically overriding, but because the category of personhood cannot be all or nothing in the way that the "pro-life" argument presupposes, and furthermore because the kind of "life" at stake is not of automatically overriding value. "Choice" merely returns us to a situation in which many values, emphatically including fetal "life," are relevant. The pragmatist's concern is only to make it possible to weigh them intelligently rather than setting a social policy that precludes all choices but one before the question is even truly opened.

Beginning to Decide

Social policy should therefore aim to make a space for individuals to try to integrate the many values at stake when they actually face an abortion choice, within the broad outlines of a framework like *Roe's*. And it must be noted that achieving such a space would itself be a major accomplishment. One effect of the immense public furor over abortion—the picketing and firebombing of abortion clinics, the constant attention in the media and the widely cited pronouncements by the most extreme spokespeople—is that it has become very difficult for anyone to approach the decision with the kind of circumspection and support that are really necessary, thus imposing one more kind of social deformation on pregnant women and their advisors and intimates.

But suppose that such a space can be created. We still need to ask how the diverse values at stake might actually be integrated by individuals in their specific situations. How do we go about deciding?

It is important to stress again that the values at stake do not need to be reduced to consistency. The problem itself is created in the first place by some fundamental tensions between values, and between values of a fundamentally different enough sort that no generalized common principle is likely to encompass them all. But integrating values does not mean producing unanimity. Instead, to use a political analogy, the aim is to establish lines of communication between different values, to make negotiation and coexistence between different values possible, recognizing the differences but also acknowledging the need to go on in some kind of coherent and centered way. The aim is to gain a sense of how the relevant values hang together and where their center of gravity lies.

When that center of gravity is not clear, the task of pragmatic engagement is, in the first place, exploratory. We need to acknowledge the different values involved, even when they are at odds, rather than to deny or suppress some of them in order to uphold certain specific preselected values. Above, for example, I cited one of the women in Gilligan's abortion study who spoke of intense feelings of protectiveness for the fetus, even though she eventually chose abortion. To have suppressed either that feeling or the many other feelings at odds with it would not have served her well, even though together they make the choice wrenching. Gilligan also reveals how often we camouflage our reasons, sometimes unconsciously, in order to make them pass muster or just to reduce the tension. One woman claims to be acting for everyone—her parents, her doctor, her boyfriend—but herself. Her counselor has to persuade her that she is also, perhaps mainly, acting for herself, and then to persuade her that her needs too are valid.[23]

A certain center of gravity may emerge simply from this exploration. A second step, in any case, is to begin to articulate the connections between apparently different concerns that emerge as one explores one's values in this way. Given the current shape of the debate, we will no doubt hear a lot about fetal life and women's autonomy as these patterns begin to take shape. Still, again, these are by no means the only possibilities. People's lives are always more complicated than these very general terms suggest. Perhaps a couple have been planning children for years but suddenly find themselves with a pregnancy several years "too early." Here part of the question is how readily other things can be rearranged in order to have a child now. Kristin Luker argues that for the anti-abortion side, "unwanted pregnancy" in general would better be labeled "surprise pregnancy," with the idea that it might be seen not as an unmitigated disaster but instead as a challenge, an invitation, to rearrange other parts of one's life, to undertake something infinitely promising and also infinitely complicated that one hadn't planned on.[24] On this picture, a major part of the question has to do with one's openness to the unexpected—itself no doubt an unexpected outcome.

Yet another person might find her center of gravity not in any values immediately bearing on the abortion question at all but instead in the more general projects that already center her life. A woman committed to nothing so fully as an intensely artistic life already has a good sense of her way. Again, then, putting an abortion decision in the larger context of our lives may change its "logic" dramatically.

This kind of exploration is not simply an inventory of the values one already happens to hold. "Articulating connections" is already a kind of active reconstruction and shades over easily into *making* connections. In problematic situations, as Chapter 2 emphasized, values themselves are usually somewhat fluid. Certainly they may change in the process of trying to arrive at a workable answer. A woman may need to consider, for instance, how much having children really matters to her. She may explore or re-explore how central her body is to who she is, what sexuality actually means to her (now), and so on. I do not mean that these questions must be answered in one particular way. I *do* mean that they must be answered in some way, at least provisionally, and one may discover not only that one's answers are unclear but also that, on reflection, one wants to change them. Abortion decisions are not so much episodes, then, as occasions for rethinking and perhaps changing one's values and one's life. Some pregnant women do so alone, some with their mates, some with their advisors and other friends.

Of course there are also immediate decisions to make. Ultimately, again, on the view advanced in this book, the task is to act out of the most integrated sense of one's values that one can manage at the time. We might then think of the connected subsets of values suggested above—those centering around the potential child and around women's autonomy, but also many other alternative possibilities—as "candidate" centers of gravity, patterns of value that can draw more and more values into their orbit and acknowledge and assign a place even to conflicting values as well. The final stage is to let all of these candidates continue to work themselves out until one finally emerges as preeminent.

Recall Dewey's words: "Choice is not the emergence of preference out of indifference. It is the emergence of unified preference out of competing preferences." Here we may persistently try out different patterns of value, arguing for them or speaking from them with ourselves and with others, "trying them on." When we have to, we act. Then we pay attention to the consequences of our action. It is worth noting that Gilligan interviewed women not only when they were facing an actual abortion choice but also at several intervals afterward, clearly recognizing that the kinds of thinking and rethinking involved are continuous. The issue does not somehow vanish but only lessens in urgency.[25]

As the last chapter suggested, the kinds of thinking and rethinking sketched here are not at all mysterious. We are constantly trying to referee conflicting tendencies among our values, tendencies that often bear upon the most significant choices of our lives. The shift proposed here is simply to realize that ethical choices such as abortion choices are no different. The same dynamics and sometimes even the same values are involved. In many people's lives the abortion choice may be much less difficult than some other choices. If we cannot "solve" the abortion issue, then, we can at least try to demythologize it.

Social Reconstruction and
the Abortion Debate

So far this chapter has considered "the" problem of abortion more or less in the way that philosophical ethics presently takes it. A woman unwillingly becomes pregnant; she needs to decide what to do about it; society as a whole must decide what range of options will be socially supported. I have suggested a rough set of methods for addressing these questions that I hope shows some of pragmatism's virtues: inclusiveness, flexibility, ongoing engagement. Now we must remember that pragmatism suggests a much longer term and more social point of view as well. Another major turn—indeed perhaps the most significant turn of all—remains to be taken with the abortion issue.

Remember that pragmatism challenges us to rethink the "givens" of problematic situations themselves. Rather than taking problems as fixed and inevitable, inviting only "solution," we must consider changing our practices and institutions so that such problems do not arise in so intractable a way. Following Dewey, let us call this kind of change "social reconstruction." Chapter 2 offered as a first example the possibility of rethinking the problem of euthanasia by asking how and why euthanasia itself has emerged as problematic in contemporary life, and about what social changes might head the problem off before it even emerges in the first place. Let us now ask, more systematically, the same sorts of questions about abortion.

Making Abortion Less Necessary

The need for abortion arises most directly from the problem of unintended and burdensome pregnancies and, if they are carried to term, children. The burden is both economic and personal. Eighty-two percent of all American women getting abortions in 1987 were unmarried, and nearly all were either working or attending school. Most were under twenty-five; two-thirds had family incomes under

$25,000 a year.[26] A simple and direct kind of social reconstruction therefore ought to address the contemporary conditions that make pregnancy and children unacceptably burdensome for women under these conditions.

A full-scale proposal is of course beyond our means here, and is premature anyway. These are matters for extended experiment with a variety of responses. But some of the necessary steps are easy to recognize. Parts of the women's movement have cast the problem in reconstructive terms from the beginning, and major parts of the feminist agenda—creating the possibility of economic independence for women, securing pregnancy leaves from work without penalty, keeping contraception legal and expanding its availability—bear upon it. A few reorientations of policy have begun to follow these lines. In 1984 a Wisconsin state legislator, impatient with the perpetual deadlock over abortion legislation, organized a committee of legislators and activists from the opposed sides with the aim of working together, as far as possible, to identify shared goals and to draft legislation to achieve them. The resulting bill passed the legislature—unanimously—and is now law. Among other things, it provides money for sex education and pregnancy counseling, with the hope of reducing unintended pregnancies, and for a state adoption center and adoption hotline, to encourage adoption as an alternative. It begins to make the grandparents on both sides co-responsible for raising a child born of their minor children. It also makes protestors guilty of criminal trespass if they enter an abortion or family planning clinic with the intent to harass.[27]

This sort of approach is rare enough that we hardly even know how to understand it, even though it is also, perfectly obviously, far more intelligent than fighting one more bout of the contemporary debate about whether fetuses are or aren't persons. In a sense it is a compromise, but it is really more as if both sides made an end run, shifting what seemed to be the problem in order to avoid the areas where disagreement is too deep-seated. It is a good example of "lateral thinking." Of course, the two sides also *did* compromise, but we might understand that compromise not as the initial and central aim so much as a natural product of each side's attempt to address the other's real concerns without abandoning what is most essential in its own. It turned out that common ground was not hard to find once "the" question was put in a broader social context.[28]

There are many further possibilities. We might concentrate on making still other alternatives to abortion workable: speaking to the needs of working and professional women, for instance, by trying to reduce the practical tensions between career and family and by expanding day care, child support, and pregnancy-leave programs for both parents, and so on. It is high time that career expectations designed for and by men were challenged and revised—and for men's sake too, if we are ever to hope for the equal involvement of both genders in child rearing.

The need for abortion, then—the absolute desperation with which some women today must seek it—is not a given, not a necessary fact of life, but a social fact open to change. Indeed, it might well be seen as a social fact that is a disgrace to society. In any case, having children, or having children at the "wrong time," needn't be made such a burden for a woman in every other region of her life. The very idea of a wrong time itself might be rendered largely moot by the right kinds of social support and the sort of restructuring of single-track work and education that is overdue anyway.

None of this implies, of course, that abortion should not also be an option. Rather, the suggestion is that it is partly our lack of attention and imagination—and lack of willingness to tackle some of the structural problems of our society—that keeps it the *only* option. That pregnant women and fetuses are made to bear the cost instead, and indeed that the two should be put at odds with each other in the first place, should seem morally indefensible to both sides in the debate as it stands.

Sex and Motherhood

A step deeper into the social background of the abortion debate and larger tensions begin to emerge. According to Kristin Luker, what in the nineteenth century was mainly a debate about medicine's right to make life and death decisions has now become nothing less than "a debate about women's contrasting obligations to themselves and to others."

> New technologies and the changing nature of work have opened up possibilities for women outside of the home undreamed-of in the 19th Century; together, these changes give women—for the first time in history—the option of deciding exactly how and when their family roles will fit into the larger context of their lives. In essence, therefore, this round of the abortion debate is so passionate and hard-fought because it is a referendum on the place and meaning of motherhood.[29]

Legalized abortion is felt by its opponents to threaten not just the sanctity of life but the family, and indeed the social valuation of motherhood itself. In particular, legalized abortion lies at the core of a larger pattern of social change that demotes motherhood, in Luker's words, "from a sacred calling to a job," and not the only job women might aspire to; in fact a particularly low paid and—without the sanctity—socially disvalued job as well. It also reflects the intrusion of technological control into the family, eliminating the element of "surprise" in favor of what may seem to be a kind of arrogant intervention. This accounts for the pro-life movement's tendency to oppose not only abortion but also many forms of contraception, genetic engineering, fetal sex selection, and so on. Even people who favor legalized abortion may agree with their opponents on some of these other points.

For the "other side," meanwhile, sexual freedom is at stake, again as part of a larger pattern of values. On the traditional conception of sex and motherhood, says Luker, sexual relations are located solidly within traditional marriage, where female dependence is not only accepted but affirmed, and sex gains its primary meaning as a means of reproduction. At worst, pregnancy becomes, as it were, the "price" for sex, a kind of punishment. For the pro-choice side, however, sexual relations primarily promote intimacy and pleasure, and are authentic and proper only when the partners are *in*dependent, even if they happen to be married. Thus the invocation of the right to control what happens in and with one's own body is not restricted to the right to choose abortion. For many women, the fundamental issue is the very possibility of an autonomous lifestyle and an inclusive and socially affirmed sense of self, whatever a woman's actual relation to men or her intentions about having children may be.

Here social divisions lie very deep.[30] But these still only define problematic situations, not ultimate and inevitable conditions. One fundamental problem we might take to be this: how and in what form social support for and affirmation of families can and should be continued, maybe even strengthened, without restricting the freedom of people who want something else, and without perpetuating the forms of female subordination that the traditional family undeniably involves. Certainly, as Luker points out, many people have enormous investments in the traditional patterns. On the other hand, many of those patterns are now only shells of what they once were. Only about 10 percent of American households fit the stereotypical pattern of the traditional family (working husband, "homemaker" wife, children)—down from 60 percent in 1955.[31] Thus, it is not as though change is merely an option, a future possibility. It is an already-present reality that we need to learn to live with.

Forms of Sexual Coercion

At this level a still more fundamental aspect of "the" problem of abortion emerges. The familiar problem of abortion focuses exclusively on what to do *after* a woman unintentionally or unwillingly becomes pregnant. We must also—in fact, surely, primarily—ask how it is that women become pregnant under such conditions in the first place, and what can be done, systematically and seriously, about *that*.

One reason, already glancingly mentioned, is the difficulty even now of obtaining adequate contraception or information about its use, not just for teenagers but for anyone disadvantaged in this society, and even for many of the supposedly advantaged. Half of all women seeking abortions in 1987 used no birth control.[32] Some chose not to use it, no doubt, but we may be equally sure that lack of access is part of the problem. Even "choosing" not to use contraception has to be understood against a background of meager social support for contraception and resistance from male lovers ranging from noncooperation to active force.

Some of this could be changed by redesigning social policies. Schools, clinics, and even the media can much more effectively teach people about contraceptives and promote their use. Of course there are formidable barriers: sexual freedom is at stake here too, and the same interests that oppose abortion also often array themselves against sex education in the schools and public discussion of contraception.[33] So we have the bizarre spectacle of media full of graphic sexual scenes and sexual incitements with no corresponding education about even the most basic aspects of sexuality or its consequences. On the other hand, some of the resistance can evaporate very fast. The past few years have seen condom advertisements on national television, unthinkable only a few years before. AIDS was the motivator then, but there is no reason why a systematic attempt to link contraception education with a partial "resolution" of the abortion issue could not make as powerful a case.

I do not want to underestimate the obstacles to these kinds of policies. Still, *one* of those very obstacles is our failure to even pose the question in these terms. Powerful interests collaborate to keep such alternatives obscured. But there is no reason that ethics, following what I am arguing are its own most basic dynamics, cannot speak out, cannot even—in the Wisconsin spirit—propose some social experiments.

Other and less noticed kinds of sexual coercion are involved too. One is the very pressure to have sex itself, especially as concentrated on very young and therefore especially vulnerable women and reinforced and intensified in multiple ways by, for example, certain kinds of advertising. But this is not a given either. Historically, after all, the pressures have been almost overpowering in the other direction. Limiting certain kinds of advertising is not out of the question. More creatively, we should also begin to think about how we could affirm rather than repress the sexuality of the young, and in particular how we might affirm its polymorphousness, decentering the furtive and male-centered genital intercourse that now counts as sex for many young people and that also, of course, produces large numbers of pregnancies. Again I certainly do not mean that such a change is likely anytime soon, given the prevailing hysteria about anything sexual, let alone polymorphic, and again I certainly do not claim to know how things should go instead. But at the very least we might begin to see that hysteria itself as part of the problem. Certainly it is possible to argue, for instance, that by adopting a basically repressive attitude toward adolescent sexuality, mainstream society has ceded the shaping of that sexuality to commercial and even pornographic interests that are ultimately far more destructive, sexist, and restrictive than even the mainstream itself might offer were it more explicit.

Other forms of sexual coercion lie even deeper and seem still more intractable. Too often the philosophical discussion sounds as though abortion becomes an issue only when contraception unexpectedly fails.[34] But Catharine MacKinnon has stressed that any discussion of the abortion issue must be framed against the background of pervasive male violence against women. We must think about abortion not only in the context of rape but also of wife battering and marital rape, and in the context of male attitudes about sexuality in general and contraception in particular such that, as MacKinnon puts it, many women come to feel that it is less costly "to risk an undesired, often painful, traumatic, dangerous, sometimes illegal, and potentially life-threatening procedure [abortion] than to protect themselves in advance."[35] The fact is that pregnancy is often, in one way or another, forced on women. And when even the most rudimentary kinds of respect are routinely denied women, social hypersensitivity to the much more problematic rights of the fetus may seem only a vicious joke. Abortion in this context becomes one small means of empowerment, partial and full of risks but still sometimes crucial.

The question raised here is ultimately the question of misogyny itself. As a society we are only beginning to confront the pervasiveness of "domestic violence"—itself a euphemism for the wife beating and child abuse that, depending on one's definition, occur in well over half of all households in America. Abortion itself has been cast by some pro-life feminists as a subtly misogynist tool. Abortion, they say, allows male lovers to avoid the consequences of their own sexuality by pressuring their lovers into abortions. Abortion "allows women to become 'unpregnant' at will, so that they can be accepted in a man's world, while men can go on ignoring the need to accept and accommodate women, their pregnancies included."[36] In any case, none of the constant reminders of physical insecurity and the multiple forms of objectification that force themselves upon women from city billboards and everyday slang would be changed even if abortion became every woman's ironclad right tomorrow. The underlying issue is clearly a much broader one. Feminist theory has begun to explore some of the reasons that misogyny is so deep-seated, but it is certainly no easy question. All of this may indeed make fundamental change in the near future seem unlikely. Nonetheless, the connection must at least be named. Even these very general and long-term projects, rethinking and resisting misogyny itself, are vital to any finally livable resolution of "the" abortion issue.

Of course everything I have said here represents only the barest beginning toward the rethinking and reconstruction that are necessary. But we have perhaps taken the first step: breaking free of the givens that frame and circumscribe "the" debate as it is presently offered to us, both by philosophers and by the familiar popular movements. That debate is but one strand in a much larger fabric. It is time to pay attention to the whole pattern.

Chapter 4

Other Animals

"Speciesism"

DRAWING all-or-nothing lines at the beginning and end of human life may seem necessary, but we at least remain aware of some of the continuities thus sundered. An even more radical division between humans and all the other animals, however, has usually seemed perfectly natural, even a division so radical that the word "animal" itself is typically reserved for the *other* animals. The effects of this moral isolation are also extreme. Commercially raised chickens spend their whole lives in cages too small to allow them even to turn around, much less spread their wings or fly, or in huge sheds holding tens of thousands of birds, so large that all social structure breaks down and the birds have to be debeaked (actually have their beaks cut off) so that they will not kill each other in their fury and confusion. Calves meant for veal are deprived of iron, exercise, even light. The safety of new household chemicals, cosmetics, and pharmaceuticals is still routinely tested, in some companies and universities, at the cost of the eyes, lungs, freedom, and often lives of test animals—rabbits, dogs, cats, rats.[1]

Most of us feel a certain unease at such practices. But it has also been easy to dismiss that unease. To worry about the other animals is supposed to be "just sentimental." To empathize with their pain is supposed to "anthropomorphize" them. Since it is fairly easy to argue that (most) other animals are not persons, strictly speaking, arguments for animal "rights" tend to be dismissed by established political philosophies that tie rights to personhood. There are also still people who believe that other animals are "just machines," that other animals do not even feel pain. Even people who recognize other animals as sentient creatures may seriously question the character and range of animals' consciousness.

For a number of reasons, then, our tradition seems to exclude other animals from serious ethical consideration. Only "we"—only humans—are supposed to count. It is this species-based exclusion that is now labeled "speciesism"—a term coined by Richard Ryder and popularized in particular by Peter Singer's book *Animal Liberation*. More precisely, speciesism is the supposition that we can draw an ethical distinction between all the members of one species and all the members of all other species on account of the difference in species itself. According to the speciesist, it is *because we are human* that we are entitled to ethical consideration; because other animals are not human, they are not so entitled. Human-centered speciesism is by no means the only conceivable kind of speciesism, of course, but, not surprisingly, it is the only kind that tempts us.[2]

Critiques of Speciesism

Can speciesism be justified? In at least one way it is easy to see that it cannot. It is not true that only humans can be "persons." Certainly we can imagine extraterrestrial beings who are also persons, if only by imagining them to be like ourselves in every respect except genetically. They must count ethically, since we do, but they would belong not only to a different species but to an entirely different biological order.

Perhaps, though, this argument at once proves too much and too little. Too much, because no alien, even if biologically very similar to us, would share the history, the practices, the socially constituted values that make us who we are. The argument makes bridging the species gap seem far too easy. It is more to the point to remember how difficult humans have found it to carry respect across mere cultural differences, like the difference between European culture and native cultures in America or Africa. The first European explorers could comprehend Native Americans only as potential slaves or circus attractions. We can hardly be sure that we would recognize a truly alien person even if it were face to face with us, so to speak, and going to extraordinary lengths to try to reach us.[3]

In any case, the argument from extraterrestrials proves too little when applied to the question about other animals, all of whom come with their own distinctive natures and integrities, and all of whom are already face to face with us. We are talking about something much more real than the imponderable possibility of utterly alien "contact." The real victims of speciesism are not extraterrestrials but co-inhabitants of the already-familiar world.

The prevailing philosophical critique of speciesism works differently. The argument begins by pointing out that some reason, some justification, must be given for the radical difference in treatment that is supposed to follow from difference in species membership. The typical characteristics of species, however—having a certain number of chromosomes, or standing at one particular outer point of evolutionary brachiation—cannot provide such a reason. Other species may have a distinctive number of chromosomes too. That humans somehow stand at a "higher rung of the evolutionary ladder," meanwhile, is only a self-congratulatory prejudice. There is no such "ladder." Evolution is more like a wildly branching bush. From an ecological point of view, *every* species fits deftly and intelligently into its niche.[4]

Consider some of the traditional justifications for the special status of humans. It is often argued, for instance, that only humans have language, and that language is so crucial an ability as to set us radically apart. The question of language will illustrate as well as any candidate the difficulties with this line of argument.

On the one hand, it is not clear that all humans actually "have language." Humans with severe enough brain damage probably understand language only as well, if as well, as domestic animals; not as well as certain chimps. Do they therefore lack all rights? (If not, why do chimps and domestic animals?) On the other hand, it is certainly not clear that only humans have language. The boundaries of language use, in short, may not correspond to species boundaries. Instead of posing all humans against all other animals, the distinction between language-users and non-language-users, supposing that it can be made precise, may divide most humans and some other animals, on the one side, from some humans and most other animals, on the other.[5]

Moreover, and most importantly, it is not clear why using language, even if humans alone do so, should make such an enormous moral difference in the first place. Because we can empathize with those beings who can tell us of their sufferings? But animals can tell us of their sufferings in other ways. The problem is not that the "beasts" are dumb, but that we are deaf. Or is it because, as Hobbes thought, only creatures who can talk can make social contracts? But many other animals live socially; indeed a great many animals live with *us*. Moreover, the implicit egoism in Hobbesian morality—restricting the range of obligation to those whose swords can be blunted by agreeing to blunt one's own—is far too crabbed a basis for constructing values anyway.

"Rationality" is another favorite candidate for both human distinctiveness and the justification of special human moral standing. But in fact rationality serves these purposes no better than language. For one thing, it may be at best accidentally true, if true at all, that only humans are rational. Other species could easily turn out to be "rational" too. In that case, on the present argument, we would have to acknowledge that morally they are on an equal footing with us. Moreover, the whole notion of rationality is notoriously vague. Defined in any specific way, it will almost certainly exclude some humans. If rationality implies the capacity to think logically, for example, then many humans fail to qualify. If it means something as loose as acting effectively to accomplish a goal, then most (all?) humans may qualify, and so will many (most?) animals. It is not clear that any definition of "rationality" will include all and only humans, unless perhaps it is deliberately concocted to do so by a kind of conceptual gerrymandering that begs the whole question.[6]

Beyond Speciesism

Some ethical philosophers conclude that at least some nonhuman animals have as serious a moral standing as humans do. The two most prominent arguments are Peter Singer's extension of utilitarianism and Tom Regan's case for animal rights.[7]

Singer argues that the only acceptable criterion for moral standing is the capacity to suffer, to feel pain. It is the inherent logic of utilitarianism to disvalue suffering whenever and wherever it occurs. There is no justification for counting the pleasures and pains of one creature and not counting the pleasures and pains of another just because the two creatures are of different species. Of course, species may affect *degree* of suffering—humans can suffer more than other animals in some ways, though less in others—but species does not affect the moral *relevance* of suffering. In this sense all species are "equal."[8]

Regan argues that some other animals are, like humans, "subjects of a life": they have beliefs and desires, an emotional life, memory, identity over time, and project a future about which they have desires. Those capacities are like (indeed, *are*) those features of personhood that ground rights. Thus certain nonhuman animals are persons after all, and have rights of the same seriousness and weight that human persons do.[9] In this sense, for Regan, some other species are "equal" with humans, for any creature who has rights must have them equally with any other creature that has rights. "Rights do not come in degrees."[10]

Both views make claims about animal consciousness that some people will find objectionable. How do we know, for example, which beings suffer and which beings don't, or how much different beings suffer? Although there is a great deal of subtle argument about particulars, the answer at bottom is very simple. We know about other animals in some of the same ways we know about each other. We can make inferences from behavior, from the cries and calls a creature makes, from close analogies between nervous systems. People who know other animals well can know their suffering just as well, sometimes better, than the suffering of other humans. To gauge degree of suffering is not easy, but we already do it in a rough way with each other, and certainly the difficulty of gauging another animal's suffering is no excuse for denying that it even occurs.

Both views are more subtle, and also perhaps more similar, than they are often given credit for. Though Singer focuses primarily on suffering, he insists in addition on the moral importance of persons, as Regan understands them: as self-conscious, autonomous agents. Persons, Singer says, may have a value not accounted for by utilitarianism, and in any case have a value that is "greater" and more demanding than the value of conscious nonpersons.[11] Thus, Singer takes seriously both suffering *and* personhood. Likewise, Regan takes seriously both personhood and suffering. He does focus primarily on the rights of persons or "subjects of a life," taking "normal, one year old mammals" as paradigms. Younger and nonmammalian animals may or may not also be "subjects of a life" or also rights-holders.[12] Most importantly, though, Regan believes that rights do not exhaust the moral realm. Suffering, in particular, has a moral disvalue not accounted for by rights theories.[13]

Regan and Singer do place their emphasis differently, and thus not only speak for other animals in different ways but also, to some extent, speak for different animals. Regan, again, focuses on developed mammals, whose minds and sensibilities are closest to our own and whose routine objectification in laboratory tests and factory farms is therefore most egregious. Singer primarily has in mind the much larger realm of sufferers, animals of all sorts that we "manufacture" by the billions and upon whom we may thought-lessly impose pain for nothing more than our own convenience, or purely out of habit. Regan is concerned with a kind of moral con-sideration that can be overridden only under special circumstances. For Singer, by contrast, moral standing just entitles a creature to have its pains and pleasures weighed with everyone else's in the great utilitarian calculus.

Clearly these are profound disagreements. Still, in some ways the similarities between the two views are, in the present context, more significant than their differences. Both views make it clear that species is a fragile moral boundary. Both views insist that merely to be consistent about our ethical commitments drives us beyond that boundary. Both views, despite their simplification in practice, attempt to honor both personlike values and sentience more generally. Finally, despite some popular misconceptions, both views also focus not so much on the killing of other animals for food or in experiments as on the violation and suffering caused to animals in the normal course of their lives. The argument is primar-ily against factory farming, drug experiments on animals, zoos, and so on: in short, against the industrial exploitation of animals in modern life. Often the death of an animal is only a welcome relief from the torments that have been imposed upon it while it lives. Both views insist that it is those torments, first and foremost, to which we must put an end.

Outlines of an Integrative Approach

Singer and Regan deserve great credit for opening up the question of other animals in contemporary ethics. Here too, however, a pragmatic outlook eventually requires us to turn critical. I will sug-gest that both views, despite their own best intentions, have the unfortunate effect of simplifying and "reducing" the values at stake rather than multiplying and diversifying them. Instead of responding directly to other animals, there is a tendency to respond first to the requirements of ethical theorizing as we presently know it. Developing this criticism will lead us toward an alternative and more pragmatic approach.

Problems with the Prevailing Approaches

Just as racism and sexism fail to acknowledge the equality of humans across race and sex lines, so speciesism, according to Singer, fails to recognize the equality of animals across species lines. But the notion of equality, as he uses it, has both the special sense and the special problems associated with utilitarian ethical theory.

Sometimes it sounds very much as though Singer is trying to deny that there are any relevant differences between humans and other animals at all. What he actually means, however, is simply that species is an irrelevant characteristic from the point of view of utilitarian calculation. Different creatures are "equal" in the sense that one animal's suffering counts the same as (is as much a disvalue as) the identical amount of suffering in another animal (though this, again, is not easy to gauge), regardless of the species of the sufferers. Stated differently, this is what he calls the "principle of equal consideration of interests," the principle that "prohibits making our readiness to consider the interests of others depend on their abilities or other characteristics, apart from the characteristic of having interests."[14] We cannot discount or ignore whale or wolf suffering just because whales and wolves are not human, or because they don't express their suffering in the ways that we do, or because (as one of my students once suggested in a moment of panic) they have four legs or no legs rather than two.

This principle, I believe, is correct.[15] But surely to establish it Singer needn't have appealed to equality, or even, for that matter, to utilitarianism. The real point is simply that other animals suffer, often very much as humans do, and there is no good reason to dismiss their suffering as unimportant or somehow not our concern. Above all Singer is trying to remind us of the simple facts of animal suffering. The most powerful part of *Animal Liberation* is not the argument beginning from equality or utilitarianism, however provocative that argument may be, but—by far—the detailed accounts of the conditions under which animals actually live and die. Singer in the end evokes our sympathy—and not just in the sense of simple sentimental feeling, but in the literal sense of "feeling together." We too are animals; we can imagine, though sometimes in sketchy and partial ways, what nonhuman animals suffer, and we then can look, from the perspective of that agony, at the relatively trivial purposes for which humans often impose that suffering, and know that it is senseless. Here ethics speaks for, and from, a much more primordial connection than philosophical arguments about equality suggest. We respond *as animals* to other animals. The fundamental need is to reacknowledge our commonality with them.[16]

Viewed in this light, the philosophical appeal to equality is unnecessary. But it is also worse than unnecessary. It distorts the very values we want to defend. Since animals are so different from each other—there is no such thing as "an animal" *simpliciter* anyway, but elephants, locusts, squids, humans—the aspect in which we are supposed to be equal becomes, in the end, an abstract construction. In a curious way it turns out to be *sufferings* that are "equal"—entitled to equal consideration—while animals actually are made *un*equal, since they do after all suffer differently and to different degrees. Sufferings come to have an existence of their own; and organisms, ultimately, are reduced to loci or "receptacles" for sufferings.[17] It also does not help that Singer has to homogenize suffering itself, so that sufferings can be added to and compared with each other in the necessary ways. By then the actual realities of suffering, not to mention suffering beings, are seriously out of focus.

These difficulties parallel some common objections to utilitarianism. Any workable utilitarianism, it is often argued, must homogenize values, to the point of typically insisting on only one. Furthermore, utilitarianism almost by definition ends by reducing people, or whatever set of beings it considers itself to range over, to loci or "receptacles" for these more or less homogenized experiences, rather than responding to us in our actual complexity and concreteness. Again, however, it is that complex and concrete response that Singer's facts actually evoke.

Similarly, Regan's rights argument has difficulties that parallel some common difficulties with rights theories. "Subjects of a life," again, are very similar to "persons": they are individuals with a certain kind of mental life, with an emotional life, memory, a sense of the future, and with "preference and welfare interests."[18] But Regan allows that a great many animals are not subjects of a life or persons in this sense and so will not qualify for rights on those grounds. Perhaps they will qualify on some other grounds, but as yet it is unclear what such grounds might be. It seems that the concept of rights has a naturally limited range. Some popular defenders of animal rights are not as careful as Regan to respect those limits, making their claims perhaps more satisfyingly inclusive but at the same stroke, as Regan himself shows, undercutting the possibility of defending them along anything like traditional lines.

But this point cuts two ways. We could as well simply say that the concept of rights does not speak for everything that is important. Indeed Chapter 3 has in effect already made this argument. The concept of personhood, and correlatively of rights-holding individuals, itself is partial, not speaking for everything that matters, even about proto- or quasi-humans like fetuses. Presumably it is even more likely to exclude essential values of other animals than to exclude essential values of protohumans.

A historical perspective is useful here. Both "rights" and "equality" are part of what Mary Midgley calls the "French Revolutionary toolkit" of moral concepts, concepts that evolved at a particular juncture of human history to speak for a certain kind of autonomous human subject, participating in the life of a moral community in certain voluntaristic and rational-contractual ways.

That this kind of subjecthood should be particularly central to the values of other animals is not at all clear, especially as we move away from humanlike animals and "normal mammals." The conclusion is surely not: so much the worse for animals. Why not: so much the worse for rights?[19]

Again, Regan does not exactly disagree. The appeal to rights was never intended to exhaust the moral universe—any more than was Singer's invocation of utilitarianism. Yet it must also be said that both views, by adopting so completely the categories of modern moral philosophy, invite this very simplification. It is no surprise that both views are read as though they were intended to be exhaustive, even when they make formal bows toward pluralism. We continue to expect that one single ethical theory is necessary. The issue raised here, then, is ultimately methodological. The conclusion from the incompleteness of utilitarian and rights theories is surely not: so much the worse for the values left out. Why not: so much the worse for any single theory about the human relation to other animals?[20]

Multiple Values at Stake

What emerges from these critical remarks are at least hints of the multiplicity and diversity, and perhaps also sometimes the uniqueness, of the values at stake with other animals. Other animals are not to be homogenized, are not simply "sufferers" or unfamiliar sorts of persons, and may not be naturally next in line for the intellectual and institutional benefits of the French Revolution. We are invited to directly articulate the multitude of values actually at stake with other animals, however disorderly and concrete and perhaps unusual those values might be, rather than to fit them into a preexisting theoretical framework with few limited categories.

We might begin by reconsidering suffering itself, viewing it as a plural and complex phenomenon. Again, rather than regarding all suffering as equal but animals as unequal in the extent to which they suffer, we must respond directly to animals themselves as sufferers, and as sufferers to different enough degrees and in different enough ways that we are best advised not to respond to them as animals (*simpliciter*) at all, but rather as individual, specific creatures, whose way of being in the world, including but not limited to their pain, is profoundly varied and rich.

As Regan points out, moreover, suffering is not restricted to pain. It may equally be a matter of the constant anxiety imposed on creatures unable to move naturally, to relate to others of their kind, or even to anticipate the occasional inflictions of physical pain. In general, the mental and social life of other animals is arguably far richer than we suspect, and the richness of this life opens up an equally rich range of possible benefits and harms to them. Perhaps, then, ironically enough, utilitarianism's single-mindedness distorts even our understanding of suffering, the one dimension that it orients all its energy against.

J. Baird Callicott also argues that suffering must be understood in a richer way, but points in yet another direction from these last arguments. What is immoral, he argues, is not exactly animal suffering as such—for suffering is a part of all life, and certainly of the lives of animals in the wild—but rather what he calls "the transmogrification of organic to mechanical processes": "The very presence of animals, so emblematic of delicate, complex organic tissue, surrounded by machines, connected to machines, penetrated by machines in research laboratories or crowded together in space-age 'production facilities' is surely the more real and visceral source of our outrage . . . than the contemplation of the pain that these unfortunate beings experience."[21] Surely this is true—only, again, there is no reason to insist that one "source of outrage" is "more real and visceral" than all others. The mechanization of the organic is *a* real and visceral source of outrage, but there are others too. We condemn industrially produced animal suffering both because it is industrially produced (flesh is "transmogrified") *and* because the animals suffer pain—and, as I have been insisting, for other reasons as well.

We can go still further. In doing so, though, we must be careful not just to draw on human models and analogies. Not only are there values at stake that go entirely beyond welfare and suffering, even very broadly conceived; in addition, some of these values go beyond values that are in any way at stake with humans. Naturally the animals most like us (or perhaps most like persons, though of course *we* are hardly just persons either) will seem the best candidates for moral standing. But then other sorts of creatures are slighted. Singer makes the slight worse by explicitly arguing for the moral standing of other animals by analogy to retarded humans and to children—as if other animals are to be welcomed into the moral world as a sort of diminished human being.[22] In fact it is precisely their difference, and the integrity of that difference, that we must recognize. Think about truly *different* animals: the exuberance of terns and gulls playing above the afternoon waters, the alien grace of a cat or a spider or a snake, the ungainly antiquity of a great blue heron lifting off. At the extremes it may be difference itself that sometimes is the preeminent value.

Grace, exuberance, antiquity, difference; and rationality (whatever exactly it is), creativity, humor, agility, delicacy, rarity, ecological importance, "the integrity of the organic" (as we might put the positive value that Callicott seems to invoke above)—*all* of these things must be weighed to some degree and at some times, as embodied in particular animals, or species, or phyla. They may be like us or unlike us. In some of these ways we may seek to be more like *them*. And none of these values are surprises. For the most part we already recognize and share them all.

Let me offer just one further and more detailed example, deliberately at an angle to the issues so far discussed, to indicate how wide a range of values are at stake with other animals. Paul Shepard holds that experience of a world of animals is necessary to the very development of human thinking as we know it. Animals are crucial to our dreams, to our art, to the development (he argues) of categorical language, in short to the very core of human imagination. We understand ourselves in animal terms: we flounder, we horse around, we doggedly hawk our wares. The first human cave paintings are stylized animals. Animals are intertwined in our taboos.

Animal taxonomies offer us our first and most compelling invitation to categorize.[23]

Shepard of course has in mind *free* animals—animals living up to their potentials in natural environments, not just distinctive genetic configurations preserved in zoos or shapes in children's picture books—and also for the most part animals of which we have some direct experience. But most of us now have very little such experience, and all of us know, only perhaps slightly below the level of consciousness, that most of the animals in our world are more closely analogous to denatured and debeaked chickens or nutrient-starved, isolated veal calves than to the free animals of our imaginations. The psychic result, if Shepard is right at all, is likely to be disastrous.[24]

This last point could be put selfishly: a diversity of fauna, and real relationships to some other animals, are necessary to the subtlety and balance of our own minds. But what is more striking here is the congruence between "selfish" and larger concerns. The ultimate point is that we are not only dependent on but are also literally part of a larger, transhuman world. Even the rationality on which we pride ourselves may not be possible without it. But to be part of the world in this way is not merely to *need* it. It is more like recognizing a home or a family. In any case, the notion that we are fundamentally separate from other animals and must find our way back to them, out of indulgence or even need, may radically underestimate our already-existing connections to them. Any serious investigation of the interwovenness of human values with the larger world of animal life is likely to turn up far more than we might initially suspect.

Some Practical Consequences

It may seem that to insist on such a diversity of values is unproductive once we turn to practice. Is not practical choice therefore made much harder—if not sometimes genuinely stymied? It is even possible that for this reason both sides in the current debate in effect collaborate in simplifying the issue, differing about which relatively simple view to take but agreeing that taking some such view is a necessary task.

In fact, however, recognizing that a diversity of values is at stake does not stymie practical thinking. For one thing, many of the values at stake often line up on the same side, strengthening the case rather than complicating it. *All* of the arguments just given—both rights and utilitarian arguments, attention to suffering in all its forms, to kinship, to "the integrity of the organic," and so on—cut against the habitual dismissal of other animals in a wide range of contexts. Some specific conclusions clearly follow. Another new shampoo or toilet-bowl cleaner cannot justify the deaths of hundreds of test animals in agony. The slow torture that is the fate of most commercially raised veal calves cannot justify the slightly lowered expense of one special kind of meat. The disproportion, the relative triviality of our "needs" when put beside the blighted lives that meeting those "needs" requires, stands out as soon as we face the facts.

Again, these conclusions are "clear" not in spite of the pluralism proposed here but because of it. The suggestion is that once anything at all is recognized on the "other side," certain practices become indefensible.

Other times, of course, things will not be so clear. Certainly sometimes it will seem that the costs to other animals are lower, or the benefits to ourselves greater. Mustn't pragmatism give an equivocal answer at least here?

Not necessarily. It would be better to rethink our expectations. Remember that pragmatism's emphasis is not so much on finding a definitive answer, right now, as it is on a continuous and critical engagement of the issues. We ought therefore to consider what sorts of decisions and practices are likely to *evolve*, given the range of issues opened up by a pluralistic approach. Consider the fact, for example, that many people who otherwise continue to eat meat are now refusing to eat veal. They do not forswear veal for their own sakes, but because it seems to them that at least this deformation imposed upon other animals is simply too great to justify the luxury of a few new flavors in our diet. But a larger reintegrative process may be set off from this starting point. Our changing view of veal is a product of better information about the treatment of veal calves. Veal raising may indeed be one of the most egregious cases, at least in the food industry. But the treatment of other animals in the same industry—chickens, for example—is not so radically different. Thus it is not such a great step to question the eating of chickens for the same reasons that we are learning to reject the eating of veal calves.

The process, then, may take time. There may well be points at which we are genuinely uncertain what to do—apparently, but perhaps only *apparently*, "stymied." In fact, I am suggesting, this uncertainty is not necessarily a matter of unclear thinking or some sort of insincerity or moral weakness. Uncertainty in the short run may be a sign not of a fundamental equivocation but of a process of reintegration that may be far more stable and intelligent in the long run. In general, again, an integrative approach shifts our attention away from the kind of "moral geometry" that expects to find a universally applicable answer now, and toward an understanding of values *in process*. That pragmatism gives us the resources to recognize, affirm, and engage such a process is precisely what we should ask.

These last points are crucial when we come to the really hard cases, cases where the diverse values at stake do not line up together but really do conflict in fundamental ways. What about programs that aim to reduce the numbers of common species of animals in order to save the habitat of rare species? Here the ecological values of certain animals seem to conflict with the individual values of others. What about cultures in which the only real source of food for much of the year is other animals (such as the Inuit culture, where fish and aquatic mammals such as seals and whales are essential)? Even the familiar challenge—what if a certain vital but potentially fatal drug can only be tested on humans or on, say, rats?—is at least occasionally a real question; even granted that rat suffering also counts, "equally" in Singer's peculiar sense; even granted that often such drugs are not at all so vital nor such tests at all so necessary; and even granted that the unavailability of other testing options is itself partly a product of our dismissal of other animals in the first place. These are important critical points, and they do change the usual picture quite dramatically, but the possibility that such experiments may nonetheless sometimes seem necessary still remains.

Here again, as with the abortion issue, it seems to me that the only good answer is "it depends." Again, though, strong conclusions remain possible. Some animal experiments and the production of at least some kinds of meat, as I have just argued, are emphatically ruled out. Our persistent habit of justifying the use of other animals without considering whether the alleged needs for that use are really real, and without considering alternatives, must just as persistently be challenged. On the other hand, a pragmatic approach does and must also leave a space for the justification of some animal experiments, and perhaps even the use (though maybe not "production," as we shall see) of some animals for food. Any approach that requires us to weigh together a wide range of values must do this. Any approach flexible enough to respond to the enormous variety of situations in which we in fact find ourselves must do this. The thousandth replication of an unimportant result for undergraduates' practice is not the same as the first tests of a desperately needed new drug, though even in the latter case there may be better options than testing on other animals. Eating fish for survival is not at all the same as eating veal for pleasure. Neither "side," and no kind of intelligence, is served by running these different kinds of cases together.[25]

We may have to strike compromises. Though neither side in the current debate may be pleased with this outcome, it seems to me that the last thing we should want is an approach that insists on one value or one type of decision in all situations. It is always tempting to respond to difficult cases by finding some simple ethical rule and insisting on it. Faced with the careless dismissal and wide-scale exploitation of other animals in contemporary industrial societies, it is certainly tempting to issue blanket condemnations; and faced with blanket condemnations and backed by the weight of established practice, it is certainly tempting to respond with blanket defenses. Nonetheless, the issue is difficult precisely because here a variety of different values conflict, and surely an adequate ethic must begin with an appreciation of that fact. Nor is there any easy or comfortable way to trade them off or any exact way to weigh them against each other. Again, a process of engagement rather than an insistence on certain conclusions ought to be our prime concern now.[26]

We could advance this point against a more sweeping cultural background as well. Since the values of (human) persons are now well developed, the rootedness of those values in a wide variety of practices and social institutions can easily be overlooked. We forget that the values of persons depend in crucial ways on the development of individuality, for example, which itself depends on certain sweeping cultural developments such as the French Revolution, the Reformation, and the rise of capitalism. But the ethical consideration of other animals, one might suggest, is at a very early stage of development (or, perhaps, redevelopment). Though there is near unanimity across our culture, for example, about the values of human persons (however often dishonored), there is no such agreement about the values of other animals. Our response to the very idea is often some form of ridicule. I want to stress, then, that in some ways the main task at present is just to keep these questions *open*. Just that: to keep us from dodging those perhaps-uncomfortable questions and therefore failing to consider other animals at all. *That*—not some doctrine about how other animals ought in all cases to be considered—is the true "animal liberation," of the present. It may be far too early to claim to know exactly how other animals should count ethically. We may have to struggle toward such an ethics just as slowly and unpredictably as we struggled toward an ethic of (human) persons.[27]

Reconstructing the Human Relation to Other Animals

So far this chapter has considered "the" question of other animals in the way that popular ethics presently takes it. There are supposed to be direct and more or less inevitable conflicts between human needs and animal welfare, and the supposed task of ethics is to decide for one side or the other, or maybe to arrange some sort of compromise, but in any case to settle matters and sort out the conflicting claims. This sorting or reintegration may take time, but it is still pictured as a response to a problem that itself is taken as given.

But in truth it is *not* given—not in the long run, and not even, often, in the short run. For one thing, there are alternatives, right now, and arguably better alternatives, to many of the ways in which we think we have to use animals to satisfy human needs. Instead of tearing our robes and resigning ourselves to sorting out "inevitable" conflicts, we might be able to sidestep the supposed conflicts completely. Still more fundamentally, we might also begin to reshape the entire relation between humans and other animals so that real ethical community between humans and other animals begins to emerge. But then the task will seem very different from sorting out competing claims between "us" and "them." These, then, are reconstructive possibilities; they at least must be outlined here.

Alternatives to the Exploitation of Other Animals

There are, in the first place, alternatives both to eating other animals and to using other animals in product testing and the like. I will argue that these alternatives are preferable not only for the specific sorts of reasons advanced by Singer and Regan but also for a much wider range of reasons. In many cases the choice between our current practices and nonexploitative alternatives is not difficult at all. The supposed conflicts, again, are not to be arbitrated but are themselves to be rejected.

Vegetarianism is the clearest case. A multiplicity of reasons besides those so far advanced suggest a largely or entirely vegetarian diet. The two leading killers in America, cancer and heart disease, are both linked directly to a diet high in meat and meat products. Meat is generally more expensive than nonmeat foods, more readily spoiled, more dangerous when spoiled, harder to digest, fuller of carcinogens and other additives, and totally lacking in many elements vital to healthy eating (e.g., fiber). Ecologically, the production of meat is a disaster. The Amazonian rain forests are being burned to produce beef for American and European markets, while the grazing of cattle is destroying the range lands of the American West. Meat production is wildly inefficient: cattle consume twenty grams of vegetable protein to produce one gram of meat protein; chickens consume ten grams to produce one gram of protein. A vegetarian diet has its own disadvantages, of course—if one also gives up dairy products, getting the necessary nutrients takes some careful planning; in general, cooking can take somewhat longer and requires more foresight, though even this needn't be true—but they are not even in the same ballpark as the disadvantages of a meat diet.[28]

Alternative product testing and teaching methods are also readily available and again are often preferable on a variety of grounds. Computer models of the human organism are in many cases as reliable for drug and chemical testing as animal bodies. Remember that other animals are not always so reliable as guides to the human organism either. Thalidomide, for example, was extensively tested on other animals without producing any of the side effects it was later found to cause in humans. Even better for some products may be testing on human tissue cultures, which are essentially just masses of cells reproduced from single human cells. For teaching purposes, both computer models and actual physical models (e.g., for dissection) are already in use.[29]

Alternatives could be developed further. We ought to recognize that the lack of fully developed alternatives (so far as there actually *is* such a lack) is at least in part a product of the ease with which testing has hitherto been allowed on animals. That alternatives may be lacking in some cases now, in other words, is not a kind of given, but essentially is a consequence of our own previous dismissal of other animals. It is also a challenge to develop alternatives. Paradoxically, although advocates of animal rights are often accused of having an "unscientific" attitude, it seems strikingly unscientific to insist that there are no alternatives to animal testing. What speaks here is not knowledge but only lack of imagination, even lack of interest.

Again, moreover, animal testing has a range of deficiencies (cost, time, imperfect applicability of results to humans) that alternatives might correct. Thus, rather than another round of the current radically polarized debate—animal-rights activists being labeled "anti-science"; animal "users" refusing to even consider the possibility that their work has ethical difficulties, partly because it seems to them that their research may be closed down as a result— a pragmatic approach suggests that it would be better to try to work together, particularly in order to perfect already-available alternatives. A few small-scale examples of such cooperation already exist, especially on university animal-use committees, but true social reconstruction requires cooperation on a much larger and more persistent scale.[30]

A certain freeing of the imagination is also implied by the shift of attention toward alternatives. For example, we might reapproach the issue of the use of animals for teaching purposes in a strikingly different spirit. Usually when "teaching" is mentioned in this context it means dissection, in schools and for medical training. I still remember dissecting a cat in eighth grade biology (no one asked where it came from). But we ought to ask: why "study" animals *that* way? Surely it would be better to study them while they are alive, to study their capacities, their relationships with each other, their ecologies, their possible relationships with us.[31] At the very least one might hope that "learning about animals" might include *some* study of live animals, which should already reduce the number of dead animal bodies that are supposed to be required. More of a case can be made for anatomical study in medicine, of course, although it is arguable that modern medicine is also far too preoccupied with anatomy in the first place, far too inattentive to the living person in all her manifestations. In any case, the bodies required for medical training are usually human, and ethical restrictions on their procurement are already well understood.

I do not mean that there is always a happy congruence of reasons, such that we never have to choose between healthy diets or doing good science and avoiding the infliction of animal suffering. "Hard choices" will no doubt continue to arise, and the integrative methods offered above will continue to be necessary. But likewise we must not fall into the habit of simply assuming that the interests of other animals are necessarily opposed to our own interests. Certainly we must not reduce all ethical problems to "hard choices" simply because an account of hard choices is chiefly what ethics has hitherto offered. Once again pragmatism invites an ethical engagement in a very different key.

Long-Term Prospects

Part of the concern motivating those who insist on taking animals seriously goes beyond these sorts of ameliorative possibilities. Imagine, for example, that we manage to eliminate the use of animals for food products and the testing of new chemicals on animals. In principle, at least, it seems that we still might be fairly indifferent to them, perhaps even more indifferent than we are now. We might still not take other animals seriously as co-inhabitants of ethical communities, just as we might still exclude them from actual co-inhabitation of "our" world. The human relation to other animals might still fall short of true consideration, appreciation, or mutuality. Perhaps their "rights" might even be respected—by a kind of benign neglect, as it were—but richer kinds of relationship would still be unaccomplished. New human "needs" might even again put them at risk.

Like sexism and racism, speciesism has a peculiarly self-fulfilling character. We may begin to recognize it by noting with Ryder and Singer the *industrialization* of meat production and product testing on animals. Almost all of this production and testing takes place out of the public eye, and indeed is systematically disguised (advertisements show contented chickens pecking around a farmyard, tuna jumping into a can) and sometimes denied. At the extremes, the animals simply become invisible. Whatever prejudice or sentimentality we are induced to put in the place of real experience can then go unopposed. Moreover, to make this sort of industrialization economically workable, and also psychologically tolerable for the few workers who remain in contact with the animals, animals themselves are turned into the sorts of denatured and helpless creatures toward whom at best only a sentimental kind of sympathy is possible. Here speciesism is institutionalized not merely in the sense that animals are treated as so much raw material, as so many "things," but also and most deeply in the sense that they are made into the mere sickly and pitiful things that they were from the start imagined to be.

This is why there is actually something correct, in a peculiar sort of way, about the accusations of "sentimentalism" sometimes levied against activists on animal issues. The overwhelming feeling *is* pity for the animals. But there is also anger and outrage directed at the institutions that have turned the animals into mere objects of pity. And it is true that the rhetoric of "rights" in this context can seem ludicrous. A terrorized, filthy, debeaked chicken that cannot fly or even walk around seems a poor candidate for serious ethical standing. But it is worth remembering that the same thing has been done by some humans to other humans. In the concentration camps people had to be utterly debased, and made to debase themselves, so that their captors could come to see them as subhuman. Ethical dismissal, institutionalized, becomes self-fulfilling. The fact that we are driven to seemingly "sentimental" ways of speaking is in fact the most central and deepest ethical indictment of our current exploitation of animals.

We need, then, to challenge and rethink the institutionalization and industrialization of human relations to other animals. Those who feel the brunt of contemporary activism need to recognize that the animals being spoken for are not necessarily the pitiful specimens of their daily acquaintance. The very reduction of those animals to so pitiful a state is part of the outrage. Activists, for their part, need to recognize that they may be speaking not just or even mainly against the suffering and violation of these particular animals, but for a vision of what a more "natural" life for that kind of animal would be like—that is, for some nonindustrialized creature, not already bred for the factory farm. This is not an easy matter to judge. It is also not easy to know how to approach the denatured animals that now surround us. Again, a *range* of values is involved, and they are complex and not always clear.

Speciesism gets going, and keeps going, because we have not yet (re)learned how to relate to other animals in any other way. I have suggested that this is *our* failure, but it nonetheless runs deep, and it also strenuously resists being exposed. The invitation is not, for example, to run laboratory studies of other animals from a posture of (at best) studied neutrality about whether or not, as one dolphin researcher put it, "there's somebody in there." Human beings trip over their own feet when treated with such distance and skepticism, and there is no reason to expect other animals to do any better, especially when many other animals are exquisitely more sensitive to the affective environment than we are. Not to mention that being "in there" is exactly what fully sensed creatures are *not*. We are "out here," alive in a rich and responsive world.

To do things differently, to reconstruct our relation to the other animals in a way that does not perpetuate speciesism but instead opens up the possibility of deeper connections, is a long-term project indeed—so long term that I am not sure that "pragmatic" is even an applicable label. But the project is not utterly utopian either. Despite the depth of speciesism within our culture, there are at least some resources for the recovery of fellowship with other animals. Mary Midgley, for example, points out that until very recently most humans lived in "mixed communities" with a large variety of domesticated animals, and in some cultures with an even larger variety of wild animals. This does not preclude thinking of ourselves as distinct from other animals, just as any other animal might, but it does (she argues) preclude treating other animals as though they are simply "things." "Belief in their sentience," she claims, "is essential even for exploiting them successfully."

> Working elephants can still only be successfully handled by mahouts who live in close and life-long one-to-one relations with them. Each mahout treats his elephant, not like a tractor, but like a basically benevolent if often tiresome uncle, whose moods must be understood and handled very much like those of a human colleague. . . . Obviously the mahouts may . . . misinterpret some outlying aspects of elephant behavior by relying on a human pattern which is inappropriate. But if they were doing this about the basic everyday feelings—about whether their elephant is pleased, annoyed, frightened, excited, tired, sore, suspicious or angry—they would not only be out of business, they would often simply be dead.[32]

How odd it would be, Midgley continues, "if those who, over many centuries, have depended on working with animals, turned out to have been relying on a sentimental and pointless error in doing so, and an error which could be corrected at a stroke by metaphysicians who may never have encountered those animals at all."

Midgley argues very carefully that even semisympathetic research with animals tends to miss their real possibilities, partly because of the very attempt to be "scientific." About Kohler's partially successful attempt to train chimps to use tools she writes:

> Notice . . . that tool use . . . is rather alien to a chimp's natural interests. His problems are not usually physical, but social, and his attention in a difficulty goes at once to a social solution. Thus, Kohler remarked that he had trouble keeping his apes to the task of getting the suspended bananas themselves, since their first idea in this predicament was to lead him to them and ask him to lift them down. Other experimenters sometimes report the same sort of thing as a nuisance and embarrassment to their work. But as "experimenting" is a notion nobody has explained to the chimps, what they do here is by no means stupid, and they might well think of the unresponsive humans as stupid or mulish.[33]

"When everything is geared to experimental purity," she adds, "what is going on is bound to become unintelligible to the animal, which has been expecting a normal personal approach, and has grounds for doing so, since it is in general treated with friendship." So the animal becomes puzzled and flounders—normal intelligent behavior. But of course it is rare enough that other animals are even treated with this degree of regard. "In general," as Midgley concludes, "any spontaneous, enterprising behavior on the part of an ox, dog, or horse tends to strike its owner as wasteful, stupid, or obstreperous, not as evidence that it has a mind of its own. He views the animal mainly in its functional light simply as a thing." And so, I have argued, it then becomes.

But again, there are alternatives. Konrad Lorenz consistently sheds "new light on animals' ways" and on the possible intimacies of human–nonhuman relations. Vicki Hearne, an animal trainer and writer, in her remarkable and moving book *Adam's Task*, argues that domestic animals are capable of artistry, nobility, delicacy, responsibility. She offers a vision of humans and domestic animals co-constituting and co-sustaining a lifeworld that is also deeply moral. Jim Nollman, a musician, has made a career of trying to find media of communication between species that do not force conversation into human terms from the start. He has tried to find media that create a kind of shared space with other creatures: going to *them*, usually in the wild, inviting but never forcing their participation.[34]

One has to read these stories—and probably one has to know some animals well—to get even the barest sense of what is possible. Lorenz's wild jackdaws preen his eyelids with their beaks. Hearne's police dogs calmly restrain their own handlers from uncalled-for violence. Nollman dances with whales. But to give even these stories their due, and to argue through all the doubts, would take far more space than we have. And perhaps even this way of presenting them—as ways of "showing" that other animals live in the same world that we do—partly undercuts the most essential change in attitude. We must approach them as fellow creatures before we will really be able to recognize a fellow creature in their response. Indeed, probably, before we will even be offered such a response in the first place.

Chapter 5

The Environment

The Need for Environmental Ethics

WE ARE beginning to struggle with the intimation that something is seriously wrong with our relation to the natural world. It is a little like suspecting cancer but not wanting to know. But the danger signs are all around us. Garbage dumped a hundred miles off the Atlantic coast is now washing up annually on beaches. The federal government is continuing its increasingly desperate search for a way to dispose of the highly toxic radioactive wastes that American nuclear reactors have been generating since they began operating, so far without any permanent disposal plan at all. A state-sized chunk of South American rain forest is slashed, cut, or burned every year, in large part to clear land to graze beef cattle, though the resultant pasture is of marginal quality and will be reduced to desert within ten years. And our society, affluent beyond the wildest dreams of our ancestors and most of the rest of the human race, increasingly fortifies itself inside artificial environments—we see the countryside through the windshield or the airplane window, we "learn about nature" by watching TV specials about endangered African predators—while outside of our little cocoons the winds laugh for no one and increasingly, under the pressure of condominiums and shopping malls, the solace of open space is no more.

Short-term solutions of course suggest themselves. If the seas can no longer be treated as infinite garbage pits, we say, let us incinerate the garbage instead. Rain forest cutting could be curtailed by consumer action if North Americans paid a little more for home-grown meat. Sooner or later, we suppose, "science" will figure out something to do with nuclear wastes. And so on. This kind of thinking too is familiar. The problems may seem purely practical, and practical solutions may be in sight. Environmental ethics, however, begins with the suspicion that something far deeper is wrong, and that more fundamental change is called for.

Beyond Ecological Myopia

For one thing, these "solutions" are short term indeed, and ignore or obscure the structural crises that underlie the immediate problems. Incinerating trash just treats the air as a waste dump instead of the sea, with consequences that even proponents of incineration admit are unpredictable. The only workable short-term solution is recycling, and the only workable long-term solution is to stop producing so much garbage in the first place, especially materials that are not biodegradable. But this calls for an entirely different way of thinking: for greater respect for the earth, more awareness of the dynamics and the limits of the wider world, and more insistent reminders that our children's children will inherit the world we are "trashing." And these new ways of thinking in turn call for a different way of living. Sometimes the practical demands are not so very difficult—using paper cups instead of styrofoam is hardly a major lifestyle change—but even this calls for a kind of mindfulness that today we lack. In the background is the suggestion that we need to recognize systematic ecological constraints on economic activity, a kind of constraint that is still unfamiliar and controversial, at least in America.

Nuclear wastes are an even clearer case. Even proponents admit that long after the normal operation of nuclear power plants is past, we will be left with enormously toxic waste products from their operation, including the reactors themselves, which after their forty or so years generating electricity may take hundreds of thousands of years to drop back to safe levels of radioactivity. Operating wastes are presently stored at reactor sites and in temporary federal storage areas and tanks, most of them nearly full and some notoriously already leaking. It is not obvious that there is any adequate permanent disposal method. Burying the wastes, even in the most apparently stable site, puts all future life at the mercy of geological changes, which are virtually certain over hundreds of thousands of years. Meanwhile, no state or community will voluntarily accept the proposed storage facilities, let alone have the wastes shipped, as they must be, by truck or rail, across half the nation.

Public opposition to nuclear power focuses, for the most part, on the danger of accidents: on the dangers of injury to *us*. But the waste problem mortgages the entire future of the earth. Any significant leakage would be devastating. Even very low-level leakage will cause genetic damage, not just to humans, but to all plants and animals, which over generations can have immense consequences. Again, then, our habitual short-term perspective comes into question; again an ecological point of view suggests radical change.

Finally, the devastation of the rain forests too is motivated almost exclusively by short-term and commercial considerations. Since the land can be bought very cheaply (or can simply be expropriated), nothing stands in the way of the most shortsighted and complete exploitation. The soil, however, is very poor—rain forests are self-sustaining and self-nurturing systems, biotic efflorescences that virtually run of themselves—and so exploitation is complete indeed. In ten years the land will not even support cattle. Like the bare hills of the Mediterranean, stripped of their forests by the ancients and since irreparably eroded, the land will become unable to support any life at all. And so for the sake of a few more years of slightly cheaper hamburgers we are turning the most exquisite jungle in the world into desert, and along with it threatening up to 60 percent of the world's plant and animal species, many of them unknown, with unknown medicinal and other benefits, not to mention the completely unpredictable climatic effects of turning enormous areas of the world's wettest ecosystems into the world's driest, the loss of atmospheric recharge, and so on.

Like our willingness to saddle our descendants with radioactive wastes into the unimaginably distant future, our willingness to sacrifice the unknown potentials of rain forest ecosystems to the most trivial and short-term advantage shows an astonishing arrogance toward the human future. And to recognize this disproportion is already to take a major ethical step. Merely to take our own descendants seriously might well require a different way of life. That alone may be enough to require of us a far more respectful and conserving attitude toward the earth, and certainly requires us to avoid making massive, little-understood, and irreversible ecological changes, like destroying the rain forests or leaving genetically lethal wastes to the perpetual guardianship of our children's children's children. *Maybe* the most pressing and vital interests of the race could justify such a thing. Maybe we could justify turning some of the rain forests into deserts if in some unimaginable crisis only ravaging the rain forests could save life on earth. But ten years of slightly cheaper meat does not justify it. Maybe our children could understand reactor waste left littering the landscape of the future if the electricity it made possible saved civilization from some unheard-of threat, or accomplished some great task. But the "need" to run air conditioners is the saddest of excuses.[1] Especially when the alternative is not even so serious as having to sweat in the summer, God forbid, but merely requires designing slightly more energy-efficient appliances and building houses that aren't heat sinks in the sun. Traditional cultures know how to build naturally cool houses. Only we seem to have lost the ability.

"Environmental ethics," then, urges upon us at minimum a much more mindful and longer-term attention to the way we interact with and depend on nature. It urges attention to everything from the medicinal and nutritional uses of rain forest plants to the

psychic need for open spaces and various kinds of ecological dependence of which we are not yet even aware. The implications are radical. We need to think of the earth itself in a different way: not as an
infinite waste sink, and not as a collection of resources fortuitously
provided for our use, but as a complex system with its own integrity and dynamics, far more intricate than we understand or perhaps *can* understand, but still the system within which we live and
on which we necessarily and utterly depend. We must learn a new
kind of respect.

Beyond Anthropocentrism

Radical as the practical implications may be, however, environmental ethics so pictured is, in at least one fundamental way, not
radical at all. In the sorts of arguments I have been giving, the
source of values is still finally and exclusively human advantage.
The appeal goes beyond the present to future human generations,
to human civilization considered as an ongoing project, but these
values are still—to adopt one useful piece of jargon—"anthropocentric": still human-centered. The starting point, the fundamental
source of values, is still ourselves.

It seems, at least to some environmental philosophers, that precisely this sort of starting point is to blame for our environmental
heedlessness in the first place. Start with ourselves and we are likely
to end where we started: preoccupied with our own needs and
reckless with nature's. One fundamental question in environmental
ethics has therefore been: is anthropocentrism enough? Can human-centered values justify the degree of environmental protection
and respect for nature that many of us feel is necessary? Even if they
might, moreover, do they really offer the right *kind* of reason? Can
it really be true that we should care about nature "just" for human
reasons?

No one denies that an anthropocentric ethic, properly applied,
can carry us a long way in the right direction. We will return to this
possibility more than once in the pages to follow. Nonetheless, it

seems to many environmental philosophers that anthropocentrism cannot be the whole story. Nature also demands respect *in its own right*. Listen for example to Holmes Rolston III, writing of wilderness:

> So what, if anything, is of positive value here? There is light and dark, life and death. There is time almost everlasting and a genetic language two billion years old. There is energy and evolution inventing fertility and prowess, adaptation and improvisation, information and strategy, contest and compliance, display and flair. There is muscle and fat, nerve and sweat, law and form, structure and process, beauty and cleverness, harmony and sublimity, tragedy and glory.[2]

It is not merely that certain plants or animals might provide new medicines or foods for us, not merely that there is beauty in wilderness that we and our descendants might enjoy. There are also values in wilderness that do not depend in any way on present or future advantages to humans, no matter how far into the future we look or how broadly we construe "enjoyment." Wilderness has a claim on us in its own right. Indeed there are times and places where we are only intruders. One upshot of a nonanthropocentric environmental ethic might be that certain areas should be entirely free of human presence, even the most seemingly benign human presence.

Environmental ethics may therefore require much more than becoming aware of subtle costs and benefits to humans in nature. We must begin, say some philosophers, to think of life on earth as a system that in some ways transcends us entirely, as a system that, in the words of Aldo Leopold, "was old when the morning stars sang together and, when the last of us has been gathered unto his fathers, will still be young."[3] Humans are not necessarily devalued, but we are definitely contextualized. No longer are we, like Adam, lords of creation, the reference points of the whole process, but, in Leopold's words, "plain biotic citizens." We are not even "stewards" of the land—even that is too superior a role—but simply co-inhabitants of what Leopold called the "biotic community."

Another approach puts less stress on nature as system or community and more on the values of individual organisms, species, and natural formations (this tree, this ravine, this mountain). Tom Regan, as we have seen, attributes rights to other mammals. Other philosophers attribute rights to nonmammalian animals too, and to species, plants, rivers, even entire ecosystems as well. Christopher Stone argues that even mountains can have legally enforceable rights.[4] There are still other approaches as well, other values and types of value that are also independent of—sometimes even at odds with—human advantage. But the shared message is clear. Anthropocentrism, human-centeredness, is a kind of species egoism that we must now outgrow, just as, earlier in life, we outgrow individual egoism. There is more to the world than us. Whatever exact form it takes, nonanthropocentric environmental ethics is now, on this view, a necessity.

"Intrinsic Values" in Nature?

Many philosophers appeal to ethical objectivism—belief in some kind of independently existing ethical truth—in order to develop and defend nonanthropocentric values. This appeal is much more marked in environmental ethics than in most other areas of "practical ethics." The reason may be that many philosophers believe that subjectivism is necessarily anthropocentric—a confusion, I believe, but a particularly pervasive one.[5] Or perhaps the reason is that environmental ethics has more than its share of writers who work within religious or quasi-religious traditions for which objectivism is still fairly congenial. Others may suspect that only objectivist principles, coming from beyond our present system of values, have the force to make us take nonanthropocentric values seriously. For these and other reasons, in any case, the early history of environmental ethics has largely seen the attempt to "ground" environmental values in an objectively and independently existing kind of value.

In an early and foundational essay, Tom Regan in fact *defines* an environmental ethic as a view that attributes "inherent value" to at least some nonhuman natural objects, where "inherent goodness" is an "objective property" of objects that compels us to respect those objects in themselves.[6] By "inherent" value Regan seems to mean what G. E. Moore meant by "intrinsic" value: in Moore's words, values "by themselves and not in relation to any other things."[7] Intrinsic values are defined by their independence, by *non*-relation and *non*association, by self-sufficiency. In *Principia Ethica*, Moore insists that in order to decide what things have intrinsic value "it is necessary to consider what things are such that, if they existed by themselves, in absolute isolation, we should yet judge their existence to be good."[8]

Likewise, J. Baird Callicott insists that "the central and most recalcitrant problem for environmental ethics is the problem of constructing an adequate theory of intrinsic value for nonhuman natural entities and for nature as a whole," and writes that

> an adequate value theory for nonanthropocentric environmental ethics must provide for the intrinsic value of both individual organisms and a hierarchy of superorganismic entities—populations, species, biocoenoses, biomes, and the biosphere. It should provide differential intrinsic value for wild and domestic organisms and species . . . and it must provide for the intrinsic value of our present ecosystem, its component parts and complement of species.[9]

Callicott undertakes nothing less than to challenge the very subject–object distinction, in light of quantum theory, in order to dissolve the usually assumed boundaries of the self and thus to extend the (assumed) intrinsic value of the individual self to nature as a whole. Proposed, in short, is a massive rethinking of most of the prevailing worldview—but the centrality of the concept of intrinsic values is taken for granted.

Intrinsic values, again, are supposed to be self-sufficient. They are supposed to be the starting points of an argument for respecting nature, the "first principles" from which everything else follows. They themselves cannot be justified by reference to other values, then, because they would not be sufficiently independent. They can only be justified on some still more fundamental and philosophical grounds. Traditionally, intrinsic values have been construed as divine ordinances, or as a priori truths about a special moral world revealed by intuition, or as deliverances of Pure Reason. It is not surprising that when Regan tries to ground his "inherent values," he feels driven to invoke "non-natural properties"—despite the irony of appealing to "non-natural" properties precisely in order to vindicate the values of nature.

But here the waters become choppy. No such ontology now carries a very broadly persuasive appeal. Appeals to God's will no longer persuade in a secular society—as if God's views on these matters were even clear in the first place—and certainly such appeals cannot be the basis for revolutionizing public policy. Moore's appeal to intuition, somewhat similarly, only persuades those who already share the intuition (or those who can be browbeaten into thinking they do) and meanwhile, as Alasdair MacIntyre has noted, explicitly precludes any articulate kind of argument.[10]

More contemporary and less ambitious philosophical arguments offer at best distant vistas of intrinsic values in nature. Singer extends utilitarianism to other animals, for example, but expansion emphatically stops when the capacity to suffer is no longer present. Mark Sagoff holds that we may value in nature expressions of traits that we value intrinsically in our own lives—freedom, nobility, and so on—but this too falls well short of showing that nature itself has intrinsic value. Thomas Hill, Jr., argues that the best moral attitudes toward persons—humility, self-acceptance, grace—are mirrored and promoted by more respectful environmental values. But this, as Hill acknowledges, is still only a more subtle form of anthropocentrism.[11] Some forms of what Bryan Norton labels "weak" anthropocentrism are enjoying a modest revival, while others manage to salvage a sense of nonanthropocentric intrinsic values by simply invoking them almost as givens, without offering any philosophical account of their origins or moral force at all.[12] By way of true justification, perhaps only a rethinking as drastic as Callicott's can succeed; but that rethinking, as recent critics have noted, depends upon highly speculative interpretations of quantum mechanics, and it ends by revalorizing a self writ large that seems to embody the very sorts of egoism and self-preoccupation that one might have hoped environmental philosophy was trying to escape.[13]

Intrinsic Values as Ecologically Inconceivable

What has gone wrong? It is certainly arguable—and I have argued elsewhere—that the concept of intrinsic value is overhospitable to the familiar anthropocentrism.[14] But the most fundamental problem for present purposes is that the concept of intrinsic value is structurally *in*hospitable to the sorts of values that we characteristically find in nature: the *interconnected* sorts of values for which a pragmatic approach is much better equipped to speak.

Take Moore's criteria. Immediately they seem to require that we test ecosystems for intrinsic value by isolating and dividing their elements. Remember the criterion: "consider what things are such that, if they existed by themselves, in absolute isolation, we should yet judge their existence to be good." To decide whether condors, or snail darters, or wild rivers have intrinsic value, we must ask whether they have value "in themselves" and "apart from everything else." But the most basic lesson that ecology teaches is that this is the wrong question to ask. In nature, as Rolston puts it, "things do not have their separate natures in and for themselves, but face outward and co-fit into broader natures. Value-in-itself [becomes] value-in-togetherness."[15]

The values of condors, for instance, presuppose far more than the bird "by itself." The whole system is crucial: the sun and the mountain ridges that lift the winds on which condors soar, for example, and thus call forth those great wings. As David Brower puts it, condors are only 5 percent bones and feathers, 95 percent *place*. Wild rivers, for their part, are now rare—it is partly the sheer contrast that makes them precious—and many of them also harbor species that are now themselves rare elsewhere but may be ecologically vital. Their silt feeds the marine estuaries on the coasts, thus contributing to the global cycle of life rather than settling useless behind some dam. All too familiar are stories of dam projects that have starved most of the marine life that formerly lived downstream: Aswan is only the most spectacular example. An ecological view, in short, reveals interdependence throughout the ecosystem. But it is precisely interdependence that the demand for intrinsic values is unable to articulate.

It may be objected that this argument only works against the alleged intrinsic value of *parts* of nature: condors, particular rivers, snail darters, etc. Perhaps what it shows is only that intrinsic value must be attributed to nature as a whole. If ecosystems cannot be decomposed into their elements, then ecosystems themselves (it might be said) must be the locus of intrinsic value; and possibly, since ecosystems themselves interdepend, the true locus of intrinsic value is the ecosystem of ecosystems, as it were: the biosphere itself.

But this approach—"biospherism," we might call it—is tempting only if we are so attached to Moore's criteria to try to save them come what may. Otherwise, once we recognize ecological interdependence on all the levels at which decisions actually confront us, it would not even occur to us to seek out some *other* level on which an independent entity can still be found. What follows, after all, if the biosphere as a whole does have intrinsic value? True, if you are the last sentient being ever to live on Earth and are thinking of blowing up the entire planet along with yourself when you die—a thought-experiment seriously proposed in some early literature in environmental ethics[16]—it may be useful to know that the biosphere has intrinsic value. But this is the sort of example that could only have been invented to rationalize an otherwise useless claim. The real quandaries that confront us have to do with *parts* of the biosphere, which, given biospherism's insistence on complete self-sufficiency, could not themselves have intrinsic value. Here, again, we need precisely to articulate the relations of their values to other values, to spell out their contexts and interdependence. At best, then, biospherism saves intrinsic value only to make it irrelevant. The values we need to articulate are still the concrete and interdependent ones.

Moreover, biospherism too is, in its way, profoundly unecological in outlook. We are asked to stand apart from the entire biosphere, from the entire Earth, in order to judge it. The thought-experiment just mentioned asks us to imagine that the Earth's very existence depends on our will. But ecology invites us instead to understand our outlooks as inevitably situated within ecosystems (indeed "within" the Earth itself, since the atmosphere is crucial to life and in fact interacts with and depends on life as a whole). We seek an ethics for, and as, *inhabitants* of this system, not as gods floating serenely and independently above it all and at whose will it exists or perishes. The Earth is not a piece of art or a hotel room, possessed or inhabited by beings entirely independent of it. It is our *home*, and like all homes always goes with us. We could not exist, and in fact make no sense, "quite apart" from it. Even the astronauts take the earth—its gasses, its metals, its liquids, and each other—with them when they go.

Intrinsic Value and the Devaluation of Other Values

The appeal to intrinsic values in nature, then, is incompatible with the very ecological insights for which environmental ethics most wanted to speak. And even this is not the worst of it. Let me argue finally that the search for intrinsic values in nature not only fails to speak adequately for the specific values whose cause it takes up but also devalues all other, nonintrinsic values to the opposite status of "merely instrumental." Ultimately the search for intrinsic values in nature does violence to *all* natural values.

Nature is of course a "means" to many things. It supports our very lives, after all: thus everything from trace elements to coal and gas to the air itself is sometimes called a natural "resource." Protected nature—parks, wilderness—has recreational and research uses, it delights the eye and the limbs, it offers a refuge and an escape, a place to regenerate and reconnect. But these values, so essential in actual environmental policy debates, are often marginalized by contemporary environmental ethics. Because they are categorized as "merely instrumental" values, they are often dismissed entirely, and at a very early point in the inquiry, in favor of intrinsic values, however elusive and speculative they might be. Any appeal that smacks of the instrumental is called "shallow," by contrast to intrinsic values, which, naturally, are supposed to be "deep."[17]

But by this very insistence on purity, "deep" environmental philosophy cuts itself off from most of the real policy debates. This may even be acknowledged: for "deep" environmental philosophy those debates are misconceived. But suppose instead that it is that dismissive concept of the instrumental that is misconceived? Values cannot be categorized and simplified so easily. We experience a forest, for example, not just as a "means" to recreation or "pleasure," or as a clever sort of life-support system, but as a kind of "home." To enter the woods is to rediscover our rootedness in nature, to find our bodies reawakening to the multiform environments that they evolved within. The pleasure that it gives is nothing so simple as sensory stimulation of various sorts, and is certainly not what the motorboat and snowmobile industries call "recreation." It is closer to Wordsworth's

> sense sublime
> of something far more deeply interfused.

It is hardly "pleasure" at all except in a very extended sense of that already promiscuous term. Likewise the life that it gives is nothing so simple as individual existence. We are part of an unimaginably old and evolving planetary process, in which all life is in some sense our kin, and in which oxygen cycling is precisely that: cycling. Forests are living things in their own rights, not just factories for fulfilling human needs. We are as much "resources" for them as they are for us.[18]

This sort of depth opens up within any real ethical concept or quasi-metaphor like "home." To reject such values because they are not "intrinsic," and consequently to allow them to be simplified and even trivialized by the prevailing conceptions of "mere means," could not be a more profound mistake. In fact, *these* values, and not the "intrinsic" values for which some philosophers still thirst, are the truly "deep" values in nature. Thus I am not at all arguing against "deep" environmental philosophy. But the real depth of the values at stake is not that they point *down* to some underlying and hitherto unsuspected ethical reality, awaiting the philosopher's speculum. Rather, they point *around*, to other values with which they are interlinked, to the familiar world that constantly invites us to know it better. Properly speaking, the metaphor of depth should assert the centrality of "deep" values in the system of our values as a whole, the extent of their embeddedness rather than their self-sufficiency. And it is from this point, in fact, that we can begin to outline an alternative, integrative method in environmental ethics.

Integrating Environmental Values: Toward an Ecology of Values

Suppose that we are asked to justify or explain the value of primitive hiking trails in the mountains: trails unintruded upon by "development," lumbering, or roads. How should we proceed? The approaches considered in the previous section require us to find foundational principles, probably expressed in terms of intrinsic values, from which particular values like the value of primitive trails can be shown to follow. Some will argue for example that (certain?) mountains have the *right* to remain wild. Others give up on intrinsic values in wilderness but still argue from the intrinsic value of the pleasure that humans enjoy in the wilderness. In either case, the underlying supposition is that environmental values above all need to be "grounded." Some ultimate value, some unappealable starting point, must be invoked.

By contrast, to "integrate" such values, on a pragmatic conception, is to follow out their multiple interconnections with each other and with other values. We are to look "around" rather than "down," seeking to contextualize values rather than "ground" them. The idea is to trace the relations of values as a system, thus interweaving a complex and varied set of values into a loose pattern, intricate and indeed still in conflict as it may be. Thus we might do for values themselves what the science of ecology does for the multiple forms of life: uncover their organic places within larger wholes. Indeed, I propose to call such a project an "ecology of values."

Some of the values involved are simple and familiar. Primitive hiking trails offer a distinctive kind of enjoyment. We move steadily, hear the birds, feel the wind, sit quietly, feel ourselves enveloped by nature in a rhythm not upset by cars or clear-cuts or condominiums. This enjoyment, of course, is what the appeal to "pleasure" tries to invoke as an ultimate justification for wilderness trails. But, as I have just argued, this kind of appeal misconstrues that enjoyment itself. Its value does not lie in its existence "quite apart" from other things, but in just the opposite direction. Its value arises from the ways in which it *connects* with other things, from its place in the emotional economy of our lives. We feel reconnected, for example, to larger wholes and other forms of life. In turn we gain some perspective on the daily concerns that may otherwise swallow us whole.

Also emerging may be a direct appreciation of the mountains themselves. They may be valued as expressions of freedom or nobility, as Sagoff suggests; or as refuges for wildlife; or as regions, in Rolston's words, of "light and dark, life and death, time almost everlasting." This is some of what we feel as we climb and muse, close to the huge and ancient bulk of the hills, seeing the peaks cleave the clouds above us. But then "intrinsic value" is no longer the issue. The point is not to win the mountains some sort of rights, for example, which close any question of "development." The point is rather, once again, that all of these features of wild mountains are deeply linked to other valued things. Wildlife refuges stabilize the larger ecosystem and also protect other animals, including the rarer species, by giving them a place to live free of human interference. By "expressing freedom and nobility" they draw in national history and cultural aspirations. These values in turn are linked to still others. There is no point at which the story must necessarily end, any more than there must be a point at which it necessarily and logically begins. At each turn there are just more places to go.

It may be crucial at times to follow out these connections in a fairly personal way. So I may speak of why *I* go to the mountains, or, say, of my hopes for a certain nobility or independence in my own life. At other times we need to speak of our values in broader contexts: by reference to geological stories, evolutionary stories, or human histories in particular places—what Rolston calls, in general, "storied residence."[19] Above I suggested, for instance, that quasi-metaphors like "home" have a force in environmental ethics beyond and distinct from any appeal to intrinsic values. So do other notions, like "kinship" with the other animals. Their force, we can now say, is that they situate us within larger and ongoing narratives. Their "storiedness" is a matter, once again, of uncovering more and more extensive interconnections. This is why Aldo Leopold advances his famous "land ethic" only at the end of a long diary of animal life on his Wisconsin farm.[20] Rolston, thinking of wider-angled stories, writes:

> I cannot give you an argument explaining all this history that has gone before—some logic by which there came to be a primeval Earth, Precambrian protozoans, Cambrian trilobites, Triassic dinosaurs, Eocene mammals, Pliocene primates, . . . Pleistocene

homo sapiens. No theory exists, with initial conditions, from which these follow as conclusions. To the contrary, from the viewpoint of . . . natural selection, the whole story seems some hybrid between a random walk and a tautology. . . . In that sense, I cannot give you an argument that justifies the existence of each (or any!) of the five million species with which we coinhabit Earth. But I can begin sketching nesting sets of marvelous stories: . . . [of] *Trilliums* [and] mayapples, squids [and] lemurs; . . . they each have stories in their niches, and they enrich Earth's story.[21]

We recognize kinship, and the network of expectations and appeals that it brings with it, by recognizing that other creatures have a place in a story that is also ours. In the diversity of niches we recognize a diversity of kinds of value that mirror and parallel our own too-seldom-realized potentialities. In the vast dialectic of evolution we recognize life as a whole as almost a living thing itself—and there are many who have considered it such, from native peoples to philosophers of biology—reproducing itself, growing, changing.[22]

Rolston is one of the few environmental philosophers whose work spans natural history on the one hand and ethics on the other, and often combines the two into almost a kind of poetry. Environmental philosophers tend to prefer his more recognizably argumentative ethical works, but from a pragmatic point of view I suggest that we ought to prefer the more evocative and integrative. In "Values Gone Wild," for example, Rolston explicitly invites us on a "trip" through wilderness values: "For the trip you are about to take I offer myself as a wilderness guide. Nowadays it is easier to get lost conceptually in wildlands than physically."[23] And in the adventure that follows, natural history and evolutionary connectedness emerge as the "embracing story." Rolston's imagery, then, is quite precise. Values form a system, perhaps even a "wild" system, and the task of environmental ethics is to learn our way around the system: precisely to explore and rediscover the connections, the layered contexts from personal to geological, that the traditional search for "intrinsic values" disconnects.

On the Logic of an Ecology of Values

Such stories do not wind their way toward just one single type of value. Immediate enjoyment twines together with historical depth. A broader sense of kinship with other creatures complements a deeper sense of being ourselves "at home." Such stories also do not wind their way only in a single direction. If sometimes I value my hikes in the mountains because I carry away from them a regenerated sensitivity to the breezes and the lay of the land, at other times I value those sensitivities precisely because they invite me back to the mountains. If sometimes I value the melancholy glory of the autumn because it mirrors the closure of my own year, at other times I value the rhythms of my yearly schedule because they mirror the cycle of the seasons. Interconnections work both ways.

Again, then, the task is to integrate multiple strands of value rather than attempting to reduce them to just one. Again too, the task is not unfamiliar. We know that to really explain why we hike in the mountains may take hours. Henry Beston took a whole book to merely hint at the riches of a year spent alone on one Cape Cod beach. By extension we may think of an extended webwork, finally looping back to hold onto itself: multiple arcs returning to completion, so that the summation of those arcs is a rough map of one's whole system of values. To explain why I hike in the mountains may take hours, but it is also not an endless task. The story has no final stopping point or ultimate "grounding," but grows more complete as I articulate the manifold connections between my love for that activity and the other values, beliefs, memories, and so on, that make up my self.

Such stories are in a sense circular. But their circularity is the same as the circularity of ecological explanations and occurs for the same reasons. We account for any interconnected whole, whether of values or of lifeforms, by filling out its connections, establishing a larger sense of how the system works, how it hangs together. In ethics, then, we invite the questioner or critic to join us on a kind of odyssey through values both shared and not (or not yet) shared, on a "trip" like Rolston's for example, from familiar values to increasingly unfamiliar ones. Not only is this an innocuous circularity; it is a necessary one.

The tasks of environmental ethics look drastically different from this "ecological" point of view. Notice in particular what becomes of the hitherto dreaded problem of anthropocentrism. On one level the question simply becomes one of empirical fact. Do all of our values in fact come back, in the end, finally and exclusively, to human advantage? The obvious answer is that they do not. That answer is obvious even to those philosophers who worry a great deal about anthropocentrism, since they themselves hold values that do not seem anthropocentric. The difference is only that such values don't come "grounded" in the way that those philosophers still expect, but instead come interconnected with other values, gaining their strength and their appeal from their linkages and synergies with other values, including anthropocentric values.

This is the crucial point. Part of the very idea of an ecology of values is that there are no foundations about which we might raise the question of anthropocentrism in the first place. There is no realm of foundational values with a gatekeeper so demanding that the crucial question is whether any nonanthropocentric reason can even get a foot in the door. There are only our actual values, mutually intersupportive. So if anything the real situation is more like the reverse of the kind of one-dimensionality usually feared. It is not merely that certain values are not anthropocentric. Even seemingly anthropocentric values do not stand alone, do not *simply* refer to human advantage. Although sometimes we may value nature because it evokes pleasurable experiences, there are other times when we value those pleasures precisely because they are after all natural. Neither value grounds the other; both support and contextualize the other.

In the end, in fact, "anthropocentrism" may not be a useful category for thinking about environmental values at all. One reason is the reason just given: even the paradigm cases are not so un-equivocal. Another reason is that there is a big intermediate category of values that are not clearly either anthropocentric or non-anthropocentric, or may in some way be both. We may reject nuclear power because we regard the waste products as an intolerable burden on our children's children, or because we regard the waste products as an intolerable burden on the earth. Or both. Or perhaps in the end the two reasons are not even so distinct. Concretely imagining future human generations becomes more difficult the farther in the future we imagine them, but the earth that they will inherit from us is also here and present to us now. Perhaps in this way there is a natural evolution from a more human-centered to a more earth-centered point of view. Still, though, it is not as though at some point in the process we must cross the line into an utterly new territory. Instead the same old ground changes and grows more fertile under our eyes.

The necessity of an integrative or ecological approach can be summarized in another way as well. We are often told that we must recognize our own embeddedness in nature before we can begin to recognize environmental values. For an ecology of values, however, *these are the very same processes*. As we begin to trace out the multiple stories and connections like those so far sketched—all of our pleasures in nature, our multiple dependencies upon it, our "storied residence," our kinship with other creatures, and so on—our embeddedness in nature opens up to us. It comes into focus perhaps for the first time. Recognizing that we are physically dependent upon and deeply enriched by the larger ecosystem, then, is not just paralleled by but is identical with recognizing that our values are deeply dependent upon and enriched by a larger system of values going far beyond "anthropocentrism." Again, however, the result is not "nonanthropocentrism" either, since human values remain interlocked within and perhaps even essential to the system. The best conclusion is that these categories themselves are no longer useful. Instead we might speak of relatively more or less inclusive systems of values, fully or less fully realized embeddedness in nature—and in general, once again and now familiarly, of more or less fully integrated values.

Integrative Strategies in Environmental Politics

Thinking ecologically about values is not merely a matter of using a different language of justification. It also requires invoking values in a different way in political and problem-solving contexts.

For one thing, given the multiplicity of values I have been stressing, no single appeal or argument should be expected to always carry the day. Again, rather than continue to seek one guaranteed starting point, we need to open ethical thinking to multiple relevant values. Consider, for example, Aldo Leopold's apparently simple and resoundingly nonanthropocentric land-use standard, very widely cited in the environmental ethics literature: "A thing is right when it tends to preserve the integrity, stability, and beauty of the biotic community."[24] In fact, even this standard read by itself is not so simple as it is sometimes considered. The appeal, after all, is to three rather distinct values: integrity, stability, and beauty. These values may not be entirely consistent. Not all stable systems are beautiful, and vice versa. These values may not even be so clear. Moreover—and this is my key point—this standard is in fact invoked in the context of Leopold's criticism of narrowly economic thinking about the land. It is, as Bryan Norton has pointed out, not an attempt to replace the monopoly of anthropocentric standards with the monopoly of nonanthropocentric standards, but an attempt to replace the monopoly of a single standard with a more complex view of things.[25] Leopold is not offering an ethical *theory*; only a provisional statement of *some* of the values that ought to find their place in an ecologically intelligent land-use policy.

Leopold in fact offers arguments that span the entire spectrum of types and dimensions of value. He appeals to the need to maintain the productivity of the land, to the need to preserve genetic

diversity for possible future use, to "the scientific value of un-
managed systems as baseline guides for ecosystem management," to
aesthetic values, to "the love and respect we have for wild species
and pristine places," to "the protection of cultural values which derive from roots in the human relationship to wild nature," to "the
value of nature in reminding us of our roots as evolved animals,"
and still more. The motives, says Norton, "may be human and con-
sumptive, or human and nonconsumptive, or nonanthropocentric,
or any combination of these categories."[26] Again, then, the "integrity, stability, and beauty of the biotic community," themselves
valuable for many further reasons, still remain only *some* dimensions
of value among many.

Second, we must resist the assumption that a relatively few
basic but simple values are at stake, and that the battle lines are
always clearly drawn. Here too, as this book has argued in other
cases, effective practical action requires openness to compromise,
and the recognition of complexity. This is a process that takes time
and cannot be reduced to a single decision point.

We should, for example, seek points of agreement when possible, aiming to be inclusive, rather than polarizing the debate. If we
begin by treating others as absolutely opposed to us, we generally
turn them into just that. It is both strategically wise and closer to
the truth to approach them instead from a standpoint of complex
mutuality. Norton argues, interestingly, that there is already a fairly
wide range of agreement on certain policy goals among both environmentalists, "radical" and "mainstream," and policymakers. The
general idea is "to promote a 'patchy' landscape, with as large and
as pristine wild areas as possible interspersed among areas of more
intense exploitation. Less intensely used buffer zones would be useful in maintaining the integrity of the protected areas."[27] There is
plenty of room for disagreement about exactly how large and how
pristine these wild areas might be, but the general vision, Norton
argues, remains a point of agreement and a framework for integrative policy.

Beginning with such points of agreement may seem like a "compromising" position. But within such a framework pragmatists may make proposals that are every bit as radical and imaginative as the supposedly "uncompromising" positions. Earth First!, for example, has proposed national preserves that would return up to a third of the United States to wilderness. Despite the Earth First! slogan ("No Compromise in Defense of Mother Earth!"), however, this is not a "no-compromise" position at all; it is explicitly put forward as a *proposal*. The real aim is to radically shift the continuum of options publicly contemplated toward truly massive (and, arguably, far more viable) wilderness. If the "other side" can propose no preservation at all, why advance our own hopes any more modestly? Probably neither will come about, but whatever does come about will not be framed by a vision of the "realistic" options whose terms have largely been ceded to the lumber companies and the Forest Service.[28]

Third and finally, a pragmatic view insists on more particular and specific kinds of arguments. When we speak of particular places we may even find ourselves talking about "no compromise." But here the real aim is just to keep the most shortsighted and destructive commercial activities out of this (particular) wild place. Not "no (never any) compromise" but instead "here at least we must stand firm." Where the claims are more specific in this way, rather than the sweeping and foundational sorts of claims I have been criticizing, exceptionally powerful arguments are possible (indeed, necessary) on perfectly "pragmatic" grounds. Why protect the new Alaskan national parks, for example? Here the answers are easy, and we can indeed stand firm: because the new parks are both exceptionally wild and exceptionally fragile; because the nonpreservationist pressures in at least this case are exceptionally unworthy, tied largely to the exploitation of energy resources to which there are any number of more intelligent alternatives; also, surely, because their protection is still possible. The same might be said of the rain forests. Here the nonpreservationist pressures border on the obscene.

The appeal for particular places, finally, mobilizes us as particular people in defense of what we know and cherish first hand. This too seems to be a strategy characteristic of the environmental movement in general, despite its sometimes extravagant differences in style and rhetoric, and this too we might take as a kind of confirmation of the more particularistic thinking suggested by pragmatism. Often environmental values are integrated around protecting a particular place, and in terms the place itself suggests. Only when demonstrating in front of corporate headquarters in Los Angeles or testifying in Washington are we really tempted to appeal to abstract and general intrinsic values in nature. *In situ*, the appeal is to the way this sweep of sand beach catches the wind and the waves, or to the sight of range after range of mountains stretching away to the horizon. The prevailing discourse has little room for such epiphanies, for barely articulate links of love and connection to particular places. An integrative approach, with its attention to narrative and its insistence that the necessary stories require long and careful telling, can finally let them speak in their own voices.

Reconstruction in Environmental Ethics

The integrative needs and possibilities just discussed arise, once again, within a larger social context that itself needs to be brought into focus and addressed in a more reconstructive key. Once again, then, we must take an entire additional turn with the issues raised in this chapter. We must ask whether the problems so far considered can themselves be reconstructed. Can the apparent conflicts that give rise to some of the current questions in environmental ethics be sidestepped or recast in more constructive terms? Moreover, as in the case of other animals, we must also take a longer view, asking what are the prospects for rethinking and changing the human relation to nature itself such that "anthropocentrism," like "speciesism," might someday not even arise as an issue that philosophical ethics must address. Again we can answer these questions only in the sketchiest way. But even such a sketch can be useful.

Reconstructive Strategies in
Environmental Politics

In the first place, not all of the alleged conflicts between environmental values and human needs are true conflicts. Currently we are told, for example, that there is a fundamental conflict between timber industry jobs and saving the old-growth California redwoods and the endangered spotted owl. On such grounds some timber companies have encouraged an intense antagonism between timber workers and western environmentalists. In fact, however, the overwhelming cause of the decline in timber industry employment has been the export of raw as opposed to finished lumber for milling elsewhere on the Pacific Rim. This is a corporate policy that has nothing to do with the availability of timber and everything to do with dramatically lower labor costs outside the United States. Moreover, though it is surely in the interests of timber workers to ensure sustainable timbering practices, many current cutting practices are *not* sustainable.[29] In fact, then, despite the way that both government and industry have painted the picture, workers and environmentalists to a large extent can make common cause.

Environmentalism is often supposed to pit upper- and upper-middle-class leisure interests against the allegedly more material interests of lower classes, which are said to require more environmental exploitation. We are invited to picture environmentalists as elitist backpackers trying to preserve their private playgrounds at the cost of keeping workers poor and city-bound. The reality, however, is very different. A range of recent studies and polls clearly show that support for environmentalism is not only extremely strong in the United States (in a 1989 *New York Times*/CBS poll, 80 percent agreed with the extraordinary statement that "protecting the environment is so important that requirements and standards cannot be too high")[30] but also is spread across the population, cutting across nearly all socioeconomic categories. The upper middle class may be more active in support of environmental causes, but this is apparently because of a general correlation between class and *activism*, not between class and environmental concern.[31] Moreover, the most vocal and coordinated opposition to environmentalism comes from the top levels of corporate management, so that in fact "the *opponents* of environmentalism come closer to being an elite than do core environmentalists."[32]

I do not mean that environmental issues are simply not matters of class antagonism at all. The point is rather that the struggle is very different from that between a basically anti-environmentalist lower class and an elitist environmentalist intelligentsia. I am arguing that the struggle is better characterized in quite different terms: as a struggle to make corporate power responsible. The struggle is to insist more effectively that corporations are not minimally bound free agents but exist within a complex web of social relations that impose a variety of legitimate constraints. And that is not a hopeless struggle at all, nor at all so even or so readily deadlocked. There are clear precedents, some serious progress, and even a commitment, in principle at least, on the corporate level itself.[33] This reconception of the issue thus opens up a space for progressive politics that is hidden by the current conception.[34]

Other conflicts, real enough, may be circumvented or transformed by other means. There is indeed a conflict, for example, between our habit of taking the availability of electrical power for granted and the ecological destructiveness of the major means of generating it. But this trade-off is not a kind of unchangeable fact of nature either. The very notion that we must choose between cheap(?) electricity and a less polluted environment is once again an astonishing simplification of the actual situation, and once again in service of prevailing but unworthy special interests. On the demand side, energy conservation is often strikingly cheaper per kilowatt-hour than building new generating capacity—even given purely economic values that, as currently arranged, simply ignore most of the profound ecological costs of new capacity.[35] The problem is instead that conservation measures require a different kind of approach than utilities and their regulators are used to. Again we require some "lateral thinking." On the supply side, solar, wind, and other technologies are far more promising, and not necessarily any more expensive—certainly far *less* expensive once the ecological costs of nuclear waste disposal, for example, are considered.[36]

An oppositional politics may be necessary to make some of these changes, considering the immense political and economic power wielded by those who have an interest in perpetuating the idea that economy and ecology conflict. Still, I have tried to argue that this power is often used to make those conflicts seem deeper than they really are. And in some areas we may create unnecessary opposition just by assuming the necessity of a primarily oppositional politics in the first place. Decades of mutual suspicion and antagonism between environmentalists and corporate executives, for example, may now have somewhat worn down. Parts of the corporate world acknowledge the severity of the ecological danger and consequently the need for drastic changes, for example, the need to totally eliminate the propellants that destroy ozone and contribute to global warming, even though entire industries will be eliminated or transformed.[37] Environmentalists, for their part, increasingly acknowledge the difficulty of formulating a workable regulatory policy. Mark Sagoff and others have argued that both sides would benefit from cooperation—and point out that one major barrier to such cooperation lies in the oppositional habits and rhetoric of the other side.[38] Let us save our oppositional strategies for the times and places when they really are necessary.

Long-Term Prospects

"Deep" environmentalists will respond, however, that most or all of the changes so far discussed might be made for anthropocentric, self-serving reasons rather than because we recognize value in nature for its own sake. We need only look around to recognize that most of the 80 percent of Americans who call themselves "strong environmentalists" are not in any case card-carrying non-anthropocentrists. It may seem as though few of the suggestions so far made address the deeper problem of the human relation to nature itself. At best we may achieve only a more subtle or polite form of exploitation.

But we are now in a position from which this concern carries much less force than it used to. In the first place, again, the very distinction between "deep" and other reasons is neither so clear nor so compelling from a pragmatic point of view. I have argued that the insistence on a very particular kind of "deep" value actually distorts the nature of ecological values, consigns nearly all values to the degraded status of "shallow" or "instrumental," and creates insoluble problems of justification for the few that are left. The constructive point is not that we should somehow resign ourselves to "shallow" values, but instead, again, that we should understand the true "depth" of environmental values to lie in their centrality in and interconnection with the larger system that includes all of our values. Moreover, once we do this, as the previous section argued, persistently nonanthropocentric patterns (or, more accurately, patterns of value indifferent to the supposed chasm between anthropocentric and nonanthropocentric values, patterns that blithely traipse back and forth) readily emerge. In the long run the two sorts of reasons may even converge. In any case, surely we would do better to listen for overtones of concern for a larger world even in talk about such things as "the human need for wilderness," rather than making a project of hearing selfishness even in appreciative talk of nature. Anthropocentrism sometimes lies in the eye of the beholder.

But there is a second and even more important response to the concern that the values invoked here are somehow insufficiently "deep." All along I have been stressing that what is most central to pragmatism is a *process* of engagement with certain questions, not the determination of final answers now. Again, then, we must reject the idea that "the" task of ethics is to articulate a final and complete set of principles, right now, to govern our relation with nature. No such values are accessible to philosophical reflection alone, and the experiences necessary to develop them can only be recovered in slow and painstaking ways.[39]

The real task is to hasten their evolution. But of course different people and different institutions may evolve toward them in different ways. And *one* way is from "selfish" sorts of reasons toward, say, more of a concern with the human future (of, say, one's children). Eventually then the shared Earth itself may move into a more central place as the locus of values, since the particular humans who will inherit it become increasingly difficult to picture. We might try to hasten this process, and we might try to supplement it with others, but one thing we must *not* do is condemn the allegedly "selfish" reasons to some permanently benighted ethical category—a fine way to prevent anything else from ever developing.

Some of us have been lucky enough to have experienced the value of particular places in nature in a direct, "epiphanal" way. The most fundamental problem now, however, is that these sorts of experiences are increasingly rare—increasingly difficult or even impossible—in the world we are making. We cannot escape litter or noise even in the wilderness. We can seldom stand in any powerful natural place without knowing that it may soon be subdivided for more ranch houses. The great wild birds are increasingly rare, poisoned, shot, or now, like the condor, confined to zoos; and so on.

In Chapter 4 I suggested that our prejudice against the other animals has a self-fulfilling character. We are progressively changing the other animals into the degraded and pitiful creatures that speciesism from the start imagined them to be. Very similar processes take place with respect to nature. The early Christians destroyed the sacred groves of the pagan world, thus making the "power" of certain natural places an ever more distant memory and so justifying the conviction that sacredness resides only somewhere else, not in "this world." Or consider the status of the land more generally. For Native Americans, the land itself was a living being. Leopold, again, invites us to view the land as a moral community of which we are "plain biotic citizens." Both notions are opposed to the commercial view of the land as essentially a subdividable and consumable commodity. Yet the commercial view is hardly just a "view." In most places it is *true*. It has become a self-fulfilling view, because the land has in fact been divided and consumed in accord with it. And I mean that it is "true" quite literally, just as animals on our factory farms are becoming as blighted and stupid as the speciesist imagines. It is not just that the land *seems* dead. It often *is* dead, as when a parking lot replaces woodlands, or a desert replaces a rain forest. Or the land is radically degraded, as when monoculture (growing just one crop, killing everything else with herbicides and pesticides) replaces less industrialized farms in which weeds are tolerated and insect pests keep themselves within ecological limits (and feed on the weeds).

The problem, then, is not that we have been looking at nature through the wrong glasses, as it were, where the task of environmental ethics is simply to remove those glasses. I am suggesting that the actual problematic situation is far more complex and extends into the very physical structure of the world. Our radically dismissive views of nature have co-evolved with radically dismissive and destructive practices with respect to nature. Dismissal becomes easier and even, within its own small compass, valid. Now I believe that to a very large extent we do not need distorting glasses at all. We see the world accurately. It has itself been transformed to reflect our prejudices.

Correspondingly, the ultimate task is to resist and reverse this reduction of nature—much as we must resist and reverse the actual physical reduction of other animals. It is, of course, a very long term project, and once again we may hesitate to even call it "pragmatic." To call the entire intellectual and material condition of modern culture a "problematic situation" also stretches that term well beyond any natural Deweyan use. So perhaps the necessary "reconstruction" is best called something else too. In any case, even a sketch of such a project must be left for another venue. All we can do here is invoke its spirit.[40] But this much, at least, should be clear: it is that project, and not the more familiar forms of environmental ethics with which we began, that represents the "deepest" environmental philosophy that we can presently undertake.

Chapter 6
Justice

THE PHILOSOPHICAL discussion of justice may seem somewhat remote from the discussions that this book has taken up so far. Not only does the topic itself seem more abstract; it has also become, partly for this reason, a celebrated occasion for full-fledged turns into ethical theory. Still, the discussion of justice is not different in kind from the previous discussions. For one thing, there *are* practical issues at state, although they are not as clear as they ought to be. Second, it is not as if topics like abortion or the other animals have not also been made occasions for full-fledged turns into ethical theory. Theories of personhood, for example, have also been advanced as the central or even sole touchstones of ethics. Conversely, pragmatism's doubts about the theoretical turn elsewhere presumably apply equally to theories of justice. In short, pragmatic methods should apply to the discussion of justice as readily as they apply to the other issues discussed so far.

Justice in Problematic Situations: Between the Prevailing Paradigms

It is not always clear exactly what is *practically* at stake in the current philosophical debate about justice. In part this is because much of the current theoretical work refers only to other theoretical work, especially in the debate stemming from John Rawls's 1971 treatise *A Theory of Justice*. Rawls's conception is not exactly impractical, as we shall see, but it is practical, I will argue, in a roundabout and highly generalized way. For more specific candidates for "justice issues," in any case, we would do better to start elsewhere. I begin here with a discussion and critique of some examples used by psychologist Lawrence Kohlberg in his research on moral development. We return to Rawls presently.

Kohlberg's Dilemmas

Kohlberg presented children and young adults with a series of moral dilemmas, the best known of which is the following.

> In Europe, a woman was near death from cancer. One drug might save her, a form of radium that a druggist in the same town had recently discovered. The druggist was charging $2,000, ten times what the drug cost him to make. The sick woman's husband, Heinz, went to everyone he knew to borrow the money, but he could only get together about half of what it cost. He told the druggist that his wife was dying and asked him to sell it cheaper or let him pay later. But the druggist said "No." The husband got desperate and broke into the man's store to steal the drug for his wife. Should the husband have done that? Why?[1]

Subjects discussed their answers with Kohlberg's interviewers, who concentrated on the "why" question. The assumption was not that there is a right or wrong answer in this case; rather, the aim was instead to investigate the kinds of rationales that were offered for whatever answer was given.

On the basis of this research Kohlberg proposed a six-stage sequence of what he called "moral orientations." According to this sequence, children are supposed to begin with obedience to authority (parents), progress through peer-based norms into meeting "conventional" family and eventually social obligations, and finally, as young adults, become able to rethink conventional norms themselves from utilitarian and ultimately "impartial" points of view.[2]

The transition from each of these "stages" to the next is supposed to be fairly sharp and to be driven by its own internal logic. Obedience to authority begins to break down, for instance, when children find themselves caught between particular desires to please and obey their parents and a newer value-orientation toward reciprocity, a relation lacking between children and parents but one that comes naturally when children begin to play with their peers. Soon this conflict is supposed to move a child out of the obedience stage altogether.

Kohlberg's system is controversial. Kohlberg himself eventually withdrew the empirical claim for the last stages: no subject in his longitudinal studies (tracing the development of a number of people over many years) in fact reached the supposed last stage.[3] Moreover, certain problematic expectations shaped the data from the start. Carol Gilligan noted that all-male samples were routinely used in Kohlberg's and Piaget's foundational work on moral development. Only later were females studied, but even then, when Piaget for example sensed differences between boys' and girls' understanding of rules, his response was that this difference made the study too complicated and that "it was not this contrast which we proposed to study."[4] So girls were simply left out. In fact, Gilligan goes on to argue that a very different moral trajectory is also available and operative, especially though not exclusively in women. This "different voice" she calls a "care perspective" in contrast to Kohlberg's "justice perspective." It too has stages, from selfishness through self-sacrifice into a kind of balancing between the needs of self and others.[5]

Gilligan's system too has empirical difficulties.[6] By now probably more has been written about the Kohlberg–Gilligan debate than has been written about the Rawlsian system. But the questions I wish to raise here lie somewhat at an angle to the empirical and systematic questions at the heart of these debates. Here we are primarily concerned with the question of what the practical problems of justice actually are. Dilemmas like the Heinz dilemma are candidate answers. Kohlberg takes such dilemmas to be unproblemat-ically dilemmas about justice. They are the very starting points of his research. Despite all of the criticism that Kohlberg's work has occasioned, these claims usually go unchallenged. But is he right? Could a pragmatic approach to justice issues begin with dilemmas like the Heinz case?

Kohlberg's Dilemmas as Puzzles

Such dilemmas *look* "practical." But looks deceive. For one thing, the Heinz dilemma is absolutely bare of detail. Kohlberg apparently thinks that everything we need to know about it is al-ready given in the brief description quoted above. Actually, how-ever, this level of description at best succeeds in making it a puzzle. The minute we begin to think practically about such a case, about how we might intelligently engage such a *problem*, we clearly need to know more.

Consider just a few probable complications. Questions arise, for example, from the lack of any information on the victim. Sup-pose that she *wishes* to die? The cancer may be terribly painful; it may be the culmination of a long series of struggles for which she no longer has the energy. Elisabeth Kübler-Ross has pointed out that many people have great difficulty accepting a family member's wishes to die: it seems to them to be an abandonment. Death is often accepted by the dying person long before it is accepted by those who will live on. Is this perhaps true of Heinz? Is Heinz reflective enough about his own feelings to have asked himself what his real motives are? Or is he perhaps only substituting dramatic action, satisfying mainly himself, for a sensitive response to his wife? Astonishingly, it is not even clear whether he has asked his wife what she wants him to do.

We also know next to nothing about the druggist. Why is he demanding such a steep price? Has anyone even talked to *him*? Moreover, there are natural questions about the "miracle drug" it-self. New drugs are often extremely risky and often fail to achieve what they promise, while the side effects, which often are unrecognized at first, can be horrendous. Here we have the most suspicious case of all, a new drug invented by one person, evidently not seriously tested at all, and promoted by the inventor for exorbitant profits. It is not clear that such a drug is worth taking even if one could have it free. Or maybe the sick woman should not only get the drug free but should be paid as a participant in a drug test.[7]

Many subjects in Kohlberg's studies raised all manner of difficulties—these and others—with the bare abstractions that the Kohlberg dilemmas offered them. The result, however, was that they ended up being classified as morally undeveloped, because it seemed to the experimenters that they couldn't handle the kind of abstraction that, according to Kohlberg, "mature" moral reasoning requires.[8] As Gilligan insists, however, a better conclusion is that they were too sensitive to the complexities of real problematic situations to be comfortable with such highly simplified cases. From a pragmatic perspective they are *more* "mature," not less mature, than the puzzle solvers that Kohlberg takes as paradigmatic.

Consider one other case from the moral-development literature.

> Suppose you and two other people are trapped underground in a deep mine shaft. You know that rescue operations will take three or four days, but the air supply will not last all three of you for that long. Two of you, however, could probably live long enough on the available air—but that means that one of you must die for the other two to live. . . . Should one of you be killed to allow the others to live and return to their families?[9]

Surely *no* truly "morally mature" person would be comfortable answering such a question. Everything depends on the further details. How likely is rescue at all? How likely is rescue in the specific timeframe assumed? (How in either case could the trapped people really tell?) Are there other alternatives besides one person's death? (What about meditative and other techniques to reduce oxygen consumption? Besides, who could reliably estimate air supply in the precise way imagined here?) Who are the people trapped? What is their relation to each other and to others? Without knowing the answers to such questions, we once again have only the barest kind of puzzle, not a true problematic situation at all.

Dilemmas Block Pragmatic Engagement

One might think, though, that we could still take such "dilemmas" and merely fill them out, thus yielding truly practical problems of justice after all. Stories and real-life cases could certainly be found with an appropriate amount of detail. I will argue, however, that even filled-out dilemmas cannot serve as true practical problems of justice. This is because the very structure of such dilemmas still obscures both the great variety of other values at stake, blocking in advance the possibility of an integrative engagement with them, and also precludes any reconstructive engagement, since the dilemma is presented as a given and not as a changeable situation itself.

The first point is that such dilemmas in fact raise questions that are much *larger* than questions just about justice. Consider for example a further variant of the Heinz study. Kohlberg asked his subjects in one study whether a perfect stranger, hearing of Heinz's wife, should steal the drug necessary to her recovery if there were no other way to get it. Kohlberg then compared subjects' judgments about the obligations of the stranger with their judgments about the obligations of the dying woman's own husband, Heinz. People who answered that Heinz was justified in stealing the drug but that the stranger was not were scored lower than those who answered in a way Kohlberg considered "consistent" (i.e., they were scored lower than those who answered that both or neither are justified). Fairness, according to Kohlberg, demands that the wife's getting the drug must not depend on who she is married to. What matters is not that she is Heinz's wife but simply that she is a helpless person in great danger and need. And in a situation so described, anyone, even a perfect stranger, is supposed to be equally obliged to help, or, of course, equally not obliged.[10]

Kohlberg may well be right that it is not fair that Heinz's wife be saved while another dying person, lacking someone to steal the drug, dies. One's personal relationships are "arbitrary" from what Kohlberg takes to be the moral point of view. Still, to score the "inconsistent" answer lower—indeed to regard it as inconsistent in the first place—only embodies the assumption that fairness is an overriding value in such cases. But what justifies that assumption? A perspective that honors relationship may acknowledge that an ethic of care and of special relationship is not entirely fair. But from this perspective fairness is not the overriding and ultimate ethical concern. Impartial fairness is instead only one strand in a much richer fabric. The demands of love and relationship go beyond and may even go against justice. Heinz may even be obliged to do what is *unjust* to save his wife.[11]

In short, the Heinz dilemma is not specifically a problem of *justice*. It is a broader problematic situation requiring us to integrate at least two different kinds of value (and in fact, again, as I suggested above, still others: attitudes toward death and dying, attitudes toward risk, etc.). Notice that when Kohlberg himself poses the Heinz dilemma he does not ask what is the *just* thing to do. He simply asks what Heinz should do, all things considered. But "all things" include more than justice.[12]

Matters are even worse when we turn to the question of reconstruction in such cases. "Dilemmas" by definition narrow the options to two. Either Heinz steals the drug and goes to jail, or he doesn't steal it and his wife dies. Neither alternative calls into question the institutional status quo. But this sort of dilemma could only arise in the first place within a political and economic system that requires that people pay for all or most of their own medicines and medical care, and that construes medical expertise and pharmaceutical resources on the model of personal property. Heinz, however, is in no position to raise that question. Neither is the perfect stranger, and neither are we, confronted with the "Heinz dilemma," where the question remains whether or not to steal the drug. The very notion of a dilemma itself, then, is the wrong way to pose what seems to be the basic ethical question.

Or take the case of the three trapped miners. The only alternatives left to them are indeed to passively await suffocation or to turn their violence against each other. But to focus on the specific situation of people already trapped once again obscures the more fundamental, social problem—a problem about which something constructive might be done. What are we to say about an economic and social system that in some sense "forces" people into such dangerous jobs in the first place? Is underground mining itself just, or should it go the way of child labor and press gangs? Could it be made just if the workers were somehow differently compensated? Or is compensation for ruined lungs and the ever-present danger of a horrible death even possible? These, I will suggest, are the more fundamental ethical questions. Again, though, they are no longer questions the trapped miners can raise; nor can we, confronted with the given "dilemma."

Kohlberg's dilemmas, in short, are what are sometimes called "lifeboat situations," on the model of the extreme and stark dilemmas posed by an overloaded lifeboat some of whose occupants will have to die (they think) if any are to survive. But lifeboat situations are extremely problematic as ethical paradigms. Some writers deny that they even pose ethical questions at all, let alone paradigmatic ones.[13] Perhaps at such extremes there are simply no ethical options at all. My present point, in any case, is that the really useful questions about lifeboat cases are not about what to do once the waters are already lapping at the gunwales, so to speak, but are about how to prevent the ship from sinking in the first place. In a truly just system we would not be *in* lifeboats. Thus, scandalously enough, at least from a pragmatic point of view, Kohlberg's dilemmas systematically miss much of the point, and most of the promise, of ethical engagement itself.

Rawls's "Basic Structures"

We now turn to Rawls. Strikingly, although Rawls's and Kohlberg's views are often considered to be mutually supportive, they in fact differ radically about what "the" problem of justice itself is. Kohlberg's conception, as we have seen, is very specific. Rawls's, by contrast, is extremely general. "The primary subject of justice," writes Rawls, "is the basic structure of society, or more exactly, the way in which the major social institutions distribute fundamental rights and duties and determine the division of advantages from social cooperation."[14] If the Heinz dilemma is paradigmatic for Kohlberg, the paradigms for Rawls are questions like what the basic rights of citizens should be and what forms of government are most just for particular societies. Rawls is at pains to insist that his principles of justice cannot be used to settle particular, concrete cases like the Heinz dilemma. On a Rawlsian view, the only way to think about such dilemmas in terms of justice is to ask whether the most general institutions of Heinz's society are themselves just. Rawls proposes a four-stage sequence along which his principles of justice actually come to be developed and applied. First is the hypothetical social contract (or "Original Position") that determines the most general principles of justice; then a constitutional convention gives them form for a particular society; then a legislature acts in accord with that constitution; only then can judges and administrators apply the rules and citizens follow them.[15] The second, third, and fourth stages, however, are mostly "application." It is the first and most abstract stage where Rawls finds the true *problem* of justice.

But such a problem is impossible to take as a practical problem of justice. Once again, though now for very different reasons, everything that characterizes real problematic situations in the life of particular communities is disconnected, indeed devalued. In the Original Position, Rawls asks us to imagine people coming together to decide on the "basic structure of society" behind what he calls the "veil of ignorance." This is a prohibition on knowing anything at all particular about themselves—their gender, race, genera-tion, class, abilities, and so on—and anything particular about their community, such as its particular history, its political or economic situation, "or the level of civilization and culture it has been able to obtain."[16] They are supposed to know only "general facts."

For Rawls, the veil of ignorance is a device to ensure that choices are made only from a kind of general or universal point of view. Indeed, given the structure of the Original Position, the only thing people *can* choose are general ethical principles. The restric-tion is natural enough if one believes, as Rawls and most ethical theorists do, that precisely this is the task of ethics. Impartiality is supposed to be the guiding light of ethics, and only general ethical principles are supposed to guarantee impartiality. Again, however, pragmatism represents a very different approach to ethics, a recon-structive and integrative engagement with the actual problems of our lives and communities. Impartiality, so far as we seek it, will have to be sought within such problematic situations. But this kind of engagement is simply precluded by Rawls's assumptions.

One can't even begin to reconstruct a problem without know-ing its actual, specific historical and individual context. In the ab-stract, without a specific history of engagement that one tries to extend and improve, reconstruction has no resources. But all real problems have such a history and context. It was crucial at the end of Chapter 3, for example, to contextualize the abortion debate in a particular and contemporary setting: against the background of what Kristin Luker calls the contemporary "politics of mother-hood," for example, or for that matter simply against the back-ground of a society that provides almost no support for parents whose babies may come at inopportune times. To truly engage the problem reconstructively, I argued, is to address these sorts of problems. "The" abortion problem in the abstract, by contrast, tends to collapse into metaphysical and out-of-context questions like the familiar questions about the status of the fetus. Behind the veil of ignorance, not knowing anything about our actual commu-nities and their histories and possibilities, that is all we can ask.

Integrative strategies are precluded by the Rawlsian scheme in two more general ways. First, since justice is assumed to be the primary value at stake, the question of integrating justice with any other values (e.g., environmental, historical, or religious values), even—especially—on the level of "the basic structure of society," is simply ruled out.[17] Matters are even worse on the level of particular problems, since conclusions about justice are supposed to be deduced from general principles. We are emphatically *not* invited to develop an overall conclusion about what should be done in the situation by way of integrating the particular values at stake. This, though, is a complicated matter, since Rawls himself proposes a somewhat integrative strategy on the theoretical level. I take the question up again in the next section.

To summarize: if Kohlberg's dilemmas are too bare and too specific to engage integrative and reconstructive strategies, Rawls's scheme is too abstract. And abstraction disengages our pragmatic skills just as readily, perhaps even more readily, as the reduction of problems to bare puzzles. Rawls even makes the denial of the necessary information part of his explicit method. We are still in search of the practical problems of justice.

Justice as a Question of Institutional Reconstruction

Pragmatism suggests an in-between possibility. We might take the paradigmatic justice questions to be questions on a level of generality intermediate between Kohlberg's particularity and Rawls's abstraction. These are, I think, questions chiefly about specific social institutions.

It is not that dilemmas like the Heinz dilemma are not serious ethical problems, or that ethics cannot help to sort them out. Suppose, though, that they only point toward problems of justice rather than posing problems of justice themselves. Here, arguably, the question about which we can make some progress asks how society ought to organize and distribute medical care, and in particular about how or whether afflicted individuals should be expected to pay for it. That is, it is an *institutional* question, specifically a question about what I will label "middle-level institutions." It is a question about relatively specific, historically embedded institutions, institutions already known to us, with a history of diverse experiments, succeeding in some ways, failing in others, with respect to which we may attempt a variety of improvements.

Heinz's wife's situation is indeed unjust. No one should have to suffer unto death for lack of a readily available medicine simply because she cannot afford it. But ask: against whom, if anyone, can a claim be made to rectify the injustice? In Kohlberg's formulation we are supposed to answer: the druggist. In fact we are not entitled to be so sure. Perhaps the druggist's family desperately needs the money too, or perhaps the druggist hopes to use it to develop another drug that will prevent such diseases from even occurring. Surely the real charge of injustice is against our society at large. Some social provision for those in extreme medical need is necessary, though other values besides justice also bear on how it is organized. The question is systematic and institutional, not primarily personal. Cases like the Heinz dilemma, then, are more like cases that have fallen through the cracks of the social institutions about which the question of justice is more properly and usefully raised. They are problems that arise when justice has already failed, when only desperation remains.

Notice, moreover, that justice questions so conceived invite precisely the kind of empirical and experimental thinking that I have been associating with integrative and reconstructive strategies. One striking fact, for instance, is that nowhere in the world is medical care distributed solely according to ability to pay. We have instead a wide range of mixed or mostly public systems. Why have purely market-oriented medical systems everywhere been abandoned? Do such systems in fact maroon large numbers of people? These are empirical questions with empirical answers.[18] Is there also a point at which the empowerment of the medically needy unjustly imposes upon medical personnel, or upon others who must pay for it? If so, where is that point? And how might we balance and limit spending on specific medical personnel and technologies for the sake of vastly more cost-effective public health measures, like immunization and improving nutrition?

These are real questions, and difficult ones, but they are not at all intractable. Creative thinking too is engaged. Trying to reconstruct specific medical institutions allows some real space for innovation and brings to bear a specific and vast body of experience. Since World War II most developed societies have been struggling to do so. By now we have at least some rough idea of what works and what doesn't, and also where the real space for progress lies.

I speak advisedly of "societies" rather than just "governments" here, for "middle-level institutions" include many private, community, and corporate organizations and possibilities beyond the strictly governmental. The medical system in America includes a vast array of insurance companies, hospitals, doctors' groups, private foundations, and universities as well as the Department of Health and Human Services. Innovations may arise from any part of the system. Health Maintenance Organizations, for example, began as private initiatives, often fiercely opposed by the American Medical Association and viewed by the government at best with indifference. Or again, trying to think constructively about preventing dilemmas such as that of the trapped miners leads us to think about nongovernmental institutions such as miners' unions and of union–management and worker–employer negotiation, as well as federal regulatory agencies like the Occupational Safety and Health Administration and various state agencies intended to secure workplace safety. Thinking about the abortion issue partly in terms of the desperate need for affordable day care and flexible career-track expectations should lead us to think about private and corporate initiatives as well as governmental mandates and subsidies. The "middle level," then, is an extensive and varied field.

I do not mean to claim that questions about middle-level institutions are absolutely prohibited by more traditional theories of justice. Some have been raised in the ethics literature. Bioethics, for example, sometimes raises "institutional" questions under the heading of "allocation" issues: questions, for example, about the justifiability of rationing certain very expensive and chancy medical procedures. What I do claim is that these questions are made extremely difficult to recognize by the prevailing theories of justice, Rawls's and Kohlberg's in particular. We are still left, for the most part, with either very specific puzzles or very general ethical principles. Most of the middle-level questions just mentioned, for example, are not considered at all in modern moral philosophy. Those who raise them are themselves marginalized in the field. Even "allocation" questions for the most part have been forced on bioethics by the larger policy debate rather than arising naturally from our ethical theories. The more open-ended and institutional questions posed here, then, at least run against the grain of the prevailing paradigms.[19] Correspondingly, for starters, it is that grain that a pragmatic approach insists we begin to change.

Some Integrative Methods

We turn now to the question of method. Supposing that justice questions do arise most naturally about what I have called "middle-level institutions," how might we begin to address them?

Integrative Methods in Rawls's Work

In a widely quoted passage from A Theory of Justice, Rawls writes that he seeks "an Archimedian point for judging the basic structure of society," a vantage point from which, as he puts it elsewhere, "the long range aim of society is settled in its main lines irrespective of the particular desires and needs of its present members."[20] These words suggest that ethics could, perhaps even must, proceed from a standpoint outside our actual complex and varied values, a standpoint from which we can comprehend; criticize, and, indeed, in the words of the none-too-modest Archimedes himself, "move" the world.

Surely, however, we cannot stand outside our entire system of values in this way. Inevitably certain values will be presupposed; inevitably, then, certain questions will be begged. If we carefully weed out the obviously begged questions, we will only find ourselves invoking values lying so deep that they have become part of the taken-for-granted background. The most subtle and persistent criticism of Rawls has concerned precisely this point.[21]

Rawls later essentially confirmed this general problem. In his 1980 lectures, "Kantian Constructivism in Moral Theory," he allowed that "we are *not* [my emphasis] trying to find a conception of justice suitable for all societies regardless of their particular social or historical circumstances." Instead the theory "deliberately stays on the surface"; it is intended simply as a useful basis of agreement in our society.[22] Again, "the aim . . . is to articulate and make explicit those shared notions and principles thought to be already latent in common sense; or, if common sense is hesitant and uncertain, and doesn't know what to think, to propose to it certain conceptions and principles congenial to its most essential convictions and historical traditions."[23]

By invoking "essential convictions," "shared notions," and "historical traditions," the project on this newer characterization aims primarily to draw our values out, to locate them with respect to each other, and hence to articulate them. Here Rawls does not pretend to seek an independent, asocial, and timeless judgmental perspective. The aim instead is to make sense of our values, to articulate, connect, and carry on our complex convictions. A number of different values are related to justice values without being reduced to them. In addition to justice and fairness, Rawls "locates" the values of freedom, democracy, rationality, tolerance, self-respect, self-actualization, autonomy, and others. Justice is "congruent" with rational life plans, it "combines with" the idea of social union, it "provides for" the unity of the self, and so on.[24] This weaving-together, this rich picture of a possible social life, is universally noted as one of the most impressive features of Rawls's work.

Here Rawls's method exemplifies what I have described in general as "integrating" values and in Chapter 5 as an "ecology of values." Rawls seeks to articulate our values in a connected and patterned way, weaving a number of conflicting and diverse values together into a more harmonized framework—without, however, deducing them from one single, principled starting point or reducing them to aspects of one single, narrow conception. The aim is simply to arrive at a consistent and "thick" ideal of human social life—framed, to be sure, by more abstract principles of justice, but not determined by them.

Even when Rawls takes up the question of principles he offers a somewhat more holistic way of approaching them, emphasizing the process of arriving at them as well as the end results. We begin with essential values, he says, but not as unassailable starting points. Instead, "the justification of an account of justice is a matter of mutual support of many considerations, of everything fitting together into one coherent view." We state provisional principles; then we try to adjust them to our considered intuitions. At the same time we adjust some of these intuitions to the principles being considered, when we are more certain of, or more attracted to, the principle. Thought-experiments or models like the Original Position are introduced to help clarify both principles and intuitions. Mutual adjustment goes on until we reach a stable and consistent set of principles, supporting judgments, and models.[25] Rawls calls this stable point the point of "reflective equilibrium." Probably it does not matter whether such a point is actually reached; in any case, it serves as a regulative ideal as we attempt to better bring into balance what will always be a somewhat conflicting set of values.

Rawls and the Question of Theory
If the above were all we knew of Rawls—his appeal to "shared convictions" and traditions, his seeming insistence on balancing a diverse set of values without reducing their complexity—he might

be almost a model pragmatist: a little too given to speak in generalities, perhaps, but still sensitive to our actual moral thinking in commendable ways. Certainly the search for reflective equilibria approximates the search for what Chapter 3 called the "center of gravity" of our values. Again, we begin with a particular and apparently essential set of values, then adjust them on the basis of other values, then adjust still other values on the basis of the improved original ones, and so on, until some (temporarily) stable point is reached. It seems no more than we naturally do anyway when confronted with difficult choices. The notion seems a promising one to fill out and apply.

Rawls himself, however, moves in a different direction. In the first place, he actually does much more than merely "locate" certain justice values with respect to each other. Although he does appeal to "the mutual support of many considerations," what they are expected mutually to support is assumed from the start to be a *theory* of justice, a unified and abstract account. "Reflective equilibrium" for Rawls usually implies the integration, not of specific values, but of general principles with the model used to derive them and with our intuitions about them.

Simply integrating *values,* however, does not require unifying them in this way. For one thing, a generalized ethical theory may not be possible, or may serve us poorly even if it is possible. Of course, values can *seem* to be integrated if we abstract far enough that some general principle emerges that can be made to incorporate both (all) sides of the tension. Then, however, the tension usually just reemerges in the interpretation and application of the principle. (So unjust killing is always wrong—but does abortion count as unjust killing?) Even if tensions do not reemerge, moreover, it does not follow that the theory has succeeded. Perhaps the tensions are only concealed, or are unspoken because unwelcome. It is better to be explicit, to admit the tension, and to welcome it as itself creative.[26]

It is not as though Rawls argues for the theoretical turn. As Bernard Williams points out, no one argues for the theoretical turn.[27] It is simply taken. Thus, again, Rawls's "mutual support of many considerations" is assumed to mean support for a unified and abstract account of justice. But without the initial assumption that there must be a unity to justice values, or that such a unity is necessary to practical action, it is not clear that there is any reason to adjust our conflicting intuitions to conform to any set of abstract principles, even if the principles are also adjusted as we go. At most we might adjust our conflicting intuitions to each other, when practical conflicts arise, though even here we might simply regard one pattern of intuition as provisionally outweighing others for certain purposes, not as simply obviating the others or even requiring them to change. Persistent practical problems might require a set of low-level provisional rules, but these are nothing like the elaborate abstract structure that Rawls erects.

Walzer's Pluralism

Perhaps the integrative promise of Rawls's methodological conceptions is best fulfilled not by Rawls himself but in some recent work by Michael Walzer. Walzer begins as we have, with a critique of Rawlsian abstraction. Thus, for example, he asks us to recast Rawls's fundamental question: "Even if they are committed to impartiality, the question most likely to arise in the minds of the members of a political community is not, What would rational individuals choose under universalizing conditions of such-and-such a sort? But rather, What would individuals like us choose, who are situated as we are, who share a culture and are determined to go on sharing it?"[28]

From the start the aim is to talk about real people under real conditions. This question, moreover, is a more or less empirical one. To determine what people "like us" would choose, Walzer argues, we can look to what "we" *have* chosen. In fact our choices have been complex, compromises between different values at odds: "There never has been a single criterion . . . for all distributions. Desert, qualification, birth and blood, friendship, need, free exchange, political loyalty, democratic decision: each has had its place, along with many others, uneasily coexisting, invoked by competing groups."[29] We have, in short, a plurality of justice values, regularly in conflict. Often enough, for example, different standards of justice are invoked by different oppressed groups against the system that oppresses them. But the nature of the oppression, and our resources for opposing it, differ too. "Need" will be invoked against "free exchange" as a distributional criterion when market forces produce a needy class. "Free exchange" will be invoked against "political loyalty" when political corruption and bureaucracy become too confining.

Different goods have different appropriate distributional criteria. Here lies the crux of Walzer's actual constructive method. We must look for what Walzer calls the "meaning" of the particular good in question, being careful to keep other goods with other meanings from dominating and controlling its distribution. "Dominance"—one sort of good, with one specific meaning, invading or "spilling over" into the distribution of other goods with other meanings—thus defines what Walzer takes to be injustice. It is not simply that the wrong good is dominant: money, say, as opposed to merit, or need. Nor is the problem that a properly dominant good is improperly distributed. The problem lies instead with the idea of a dominant good itself. There should *be* no dominant goods. Each good should be distributed according to its own independent meaning. Each major good has its own proper "sphere."

Money, for example, is not supposed to be able to buy votes, or love, or people. Though all the same it sometimes can, "it does so, as it were, behind the backs of many of those things and in spite of their social meanings."[30] Within its own proper sphere, though, "free exchange" is supposed to be an entirely appropriate distributional criterion. It is unjust when money buys political office, but not unjust when money buys luxury goods, even if others cannot afford them. It is also unjust when political office can routinely be used to amass a fortune. Money and political power must be kept separate, says Walzer, ultimately for the sake of both.

The task of ethics is in part to spell out such "meanings," a sociological and historical task as well. Certainly they have varied.

The Greeks believed that public drama was a social need, requiring communal provision, but that food and shelter for the poor were not. The Middle Ages took the primary need to be salvation, eternal life; the Church was the means of communal provision. Health care may now be a need in the same way, maybe because physical longevity is as close as we can come to eternal life. But need is still only a recognized entitlement in the sphere of "welfare" goods. Need does not entitle you to, say, the best education—any more than having money does (or should). Nor should lack of money disqualify. Here only ability and interest are supposed to count. Walzer cites the story of Hillel, the great Talmudic sage who as a young and penniless Jerusalem woodcutter listened through the academy's skylight to lectures he could not afford to attend. Discovered when he fell asleep one night, exhausted, on the skylight, he was admitted on the spot, all the fees waived, "he was so obviously a student." This is what education is supposed to *mean*.

Commentary and Criticism

Walzer is not trying to unify justice values. There is no single framework under which they all are supposed to fit. The concern is instead to "locate" justice values, to show how they relate to each other and to our beliefs, and to show how various societies have worked them out over time. The project requires following them in the direction of complexity and historical particularity rather than simplicity and abstraction: it is a political and historical kind of "ecology of values." It requires paying attention, as Walzer shows, to stories and folktales, to exemplary people and institutions, to established social practices as well as persistent social tensions. *This* is what it means to take seriously Rawls's suggestion that we need to "articulate and make explicit those shared notions and principles thought to be already latent in common sense," to spell out our "essential convictions and historical traditions." It is not to be done by abstracting and unifying but in a much more particular and empirical way. Walzer's methods also recall Jonsen and Toulmin's characterization of moral arguments as "networks of considerations," woven together out of a particular situation as best we can, rather than the "moral geometry" that principles of justice seem to suggest.

Walzer's method in turn could be somewhat more integrative. There is a temptation, at least, in speaking of "spheres" of values, to overemphasize the independence of the spheres. Walzer sometimes seems to divide values too sharply, threatening to *dis*-integrate them rather than connect them. But we need more than a set of disparate realms related only by contiguity. Our lives and our communal values need to make sense as a whole.

In fact, no social good has completely free rein anywhere. Money, for instance, does not have free rein even in the marketplace. Businesses are expected to make charitable contributions and arguably are obliged to act in socially responsible ways even when the law does not require it.[31] Or again, knowledge seldom exists just "for its own sake," even in the academy. Universities, particularly publicly supported ones, must serve their communities' needs, and not just by producing enough technically trained people but also by allowing other community needs to partially shape its research. Contra Walzer, we should expect and even encourage a certain degree of "spillover" from sphere to sphere.

Perhaps Walzer overreacts to a certain totalizing turn in the modern theory of justice. He compartmentalizes values partly to save the rich variety of concrete values from reduction to one or a few abstract principles. But the compartments must not be made airtight. We might propose a small change of metaphor. Think of values as falling into somewhat overlapping *regions:* not distinct "spheres," but meshing sets of concerns, each with a certain center of gravity and internal connectedness, only not so impermeable an internal connectedness and not so secure a center of gravity that no other values can even get a foothold within. Integrating values across "spheres" then, remains possible. The challenge is what it has been, according to pragmatism, all along: to weave disparate values together, even if they inhabit somewhat different "regions," to integrate them nonetheless through some line of action or some new way of thinking of ourselves that will do better by all of them than we have done so far. We still seek a larger and more inclusive "equilibrium."

An Example

For a very brief example of this kind of integrative method in action, let us consider one last time some of the issues raised by the Heinz dilemma.

In the first place, as I argued above, "the" actual problem of justice in this case is not the question whether Heinz should steal the drug, but instead what sorts of institutions (if any) a particular society ought to develop and support that might prevent such deprivations from occurring in the first place. To go farther we must now both define the question more carefully and ask what sorts of "meanings" the relevant goods and institutions actually are understood to have.

Ought our larger community do anything at all in such cases? The question is not whether society should provide anything at all that anyone happens to want. Here we are talking about a very specific and absolutely crucial kind of good: life itself, and the means to continued life. (For purposes of the example we follow Kohlberg in assuming that the druggist's drug would in fact save Heinz's wife, though as I have noted this is fairly dubious.) To put it in political terms: here at least we are not necessarily speaking about a sweeping and inclusive program of "national health insurance" (though such larger issues might arise once we ask why Heinz's wife is sick in the first place) but instead about something like "catastrophic health insurance." Or we might wish to argue for a much more systematic practice of charitable provision of basic medical goods (as for example when hospitals built with federal money are required to provide a certain percentage of their care free to the poor) rather than a kind of national accounting system to pay "catastrophic" bills. The community can act in many ways. Again, then, the question is: Ought it? And how?

I put the question in this open-ended way partly because it seems to me that political ideologies often cloud our ethical impulses when one possible implication of our ethical conclusions is that new forms of governmental action ought to be undertaken. People may agree that some particular action is ethically appropriate, but not that the government ought to do it. Here, though, this is a separate issue. The question "Ought people be left communally unprotected against 'catastrophic' medical expenses?" can be answered, at least tentatively, before we decide what form communal protection might take, should we decide that it is indeed required.

Once the question is put in this way, it seems clear to me that we already *do* believe that some form of communal provision is required in such cases. Indeed, we have already attempted to provide it, with Medicaid and Medicare programs in the United States and under the umbrella of larger programs of national health insurance elsewhere. On the private level, many doctors already expect to do a certain proportion of pro bono work (treating people who cannot pay) as a matter of course. Other similarly basic needs are also socially provided for, for example in food stamp programs. Of course, it may well be that none of these programs live up to their own standards. Some scandalously fail. But the point, as Walzer would insist, is that we do have such standards. Otherwise scandalously failing to meet them is not even possible. We may wish to experiment with new institutions and practices to try to meet them. We may never perfectly succeed. Nonetheless we do seem to be committed to try to do better.

Why do we have such standards? Perhaps one reason is this: although Americans, at least, tend to think of themselves in very individualistic terms, we also acknowledge that there are many features of our lives that are truly beyond our control. Even when we personally are unaffected, at least for the moment, we recognize that we are all susceptible to unpredictable disasters. Others just like us have been less lucky, and we can only say, "There but for the grace of God go I." Crippling accidents, unexpected illnesses, and other overwhelming health problems are among these disasters. Very few of us—indeed, in unsettled times, none of us—can count on being able to provide completely for ourselves if such misfortunes occur. Thus we recognize a kind of basic wisdom in securing some social provision in such circumstances: a complex wisdom, like most real values, composed partly of self-interest and partly of a recognition that those upon whom disaster has descended could as easily have been us.[32] "Do unto others. . . ." This, I believe, is our actual, current "reflective equilibrium." It is not a bad place to begin.

A Reconstructive View: Beyond the Justice Debate

"Middle-Level" Questions

This chapter began by noting that the problem of justice seems more abstract than the other problems discussed in this book. One reason for this abstraction is that the problem of justice is the only "problem" discussed here that is popularly named after a *value*, rather than after an actual practice, like abortion, or after a type of creature or type of reality (other animals, nature) with which our relations have proven problematic. But when a problem is named after a value it is perhaps not surprising that philosophers will take the "solution" primarily to require a thorough analysis of the value-term in question, more or less in isolation from other values and even in abstraction from real problematic situations. Correspondingly, to reconceive the problem pragmatically, we would be wise to first simply name it after the sort of practical problem actually at stake. Thus I have proposed to reconceive "the" problem of justice, less dramatically but more accurately, as a set of problems about "middle-level institutions."

Once again, then, we have asked not what something called "justice" implies about the Heinz case or about the "basic structure of society," but instead have asked questions like whether there should be a communal safety net for people facing catastrophic medical expenses. Or again, about the case of the trapped miners who are invited to kill one of their number in order that the rest survive, I have suggested that reconstructive or "lateral" thinking would address the supposed need for coal mined underground in the first place, or at the very least would consider how such operations can be made safer. The everyday risk of being trapped in such mines is itself an ethical issue, and not one about which society at large is powerless. Indeed, given the massive social and ecological costs of the coal industry, we might even decide that it is imperative to eliminate the use of coal entirely. That ethics has anything to offer the miners once they are trapped, by contrast, is not at all clear. Perhaps all we can do is try to prevent such disasters from occurring in the future.

But we are therefore left with problems that are not "just" problems of justice, at least in any of the specific senses so far discussed. In fact a full range of values is relevant to such middle-level questions. Fairness is of course relevant. But so is efficiency. So is simple affordability. So are special obligations, such as the obligations of spouses to each other, or parents to children, or communities to certain members (e.g., to those who have accepted special risks in the community's behalf), or members to communities. So is the "meaning" or symbolic value of certain acts, for example those acts that make the community what it is (e.g., voting, in the Western democracies). All of these values must be weighed together when deciding on the appropriate policies to adopt. Again, this is not to say that all of these different values must somehow just be "averaged." On some occasions certain values may prove to be more important than others—they may be more "essential convictions," perhaps—and creative new ways to honor all of them are always possible. In any case, though, "justice" alone no longer answers the question.[33]

The argument of the previous section leads to the same conclusion. None of the integrative methods endorsed there are restricted to questions of justice, nor do they in any way even bring out justice considerations as a "natural kind." Rawls's attempt to "articulate and make explicit . . . shared notions" and to "propose . . . conceptions . . . congenial to [our] most essential convictions and historical traditions" is a very widely applicable method. Likewise, the mutual adjustment and equilibration of values involved in "reflective equilibrium" can apply to almost any sustained thought about any ethical issue. Likewise too, Walzer's attention to stories and folktales, and to historical exemplars and shared traditions, is essential to "locate" and begin to weave together not just justice values but *all* of our social values. It is no surprise that Walzer manages to cover a much wider range of topics than are usually found under the heading of justice. He takes up "membership" (who has a claim to citizenship?), free time, hard work, love, political office, personal recognition, even questions about divine grace and the relation of church and state. His aim is not to expand the scope of justice questions but simply to follow out the natural tendencies of his method, which are, once again, far broader. There is a great deal more to be sorted out than "justice," though it is to be sorted out in more or less the same way.

In the end, then, the appropriate role of a theory specifically of justice is at best unclear. Perhaps it would be better to understand the appeal to justice more in the rhetorical vein than in the philosophical–ethical. Certainly the rhetoric has its uses. But that we can actually *think* in such terms, that we can usefully engage problematic situations with such tools (let alone with *only* such tools) is certainly not obvious.[34] At any rate, pragmatism insists that the "theory of justice" join this ongoing practical engagement on practice's own terms. It is not for the theory to insist that practice find a place within *it*.

Justice Talk and the Chimera of Perfection

There is another pitfall of justice talk that we must briefly note in closing. It is not an inevitable trap. Rawls, for example, mostly avoids it. But Kohlberg may not; and the popular discussion of justice, whose frame of reference traces as far back as Plato, certainly does not.

The trap is the ease with which talk about justice slips into talk about *perfect* justice. Once the language of justice is taken up, it is hard to rest content with questions like, How could the prevailing distribution of power or wealth be improved? or Should we continue to use coal? Instead we start asking questions like, What is *the* just arrangement of power or wealth, risk and reward? We begin to presume, that is, that there is but one answer, Real True Justice, something that we may dream of, thirst and perhaps even die for, or fight a revolution in the name of, that in any case is not just an improvement, not merely an amelioration of present injustice, but, well, Utopia. It is easy to get carried away.

The origins of what we might dub "Utopian Justice" (I will label it with a capital "J": Justice) are complex and fascinating, but another story. Here we can only recognize how misleading and disabling this conception is. In the first place, combined with ethical theory's tendency to treat simple principles as the only "true" expression of values, the result is almost inevitably some wildly simplified formula for "true" Justice, like "To each according to their needs; from each according to their ability" or "From each as they choose; to each as they are chosen."[35] All other values are then ignored; one may even make a virtue of ignoring them. If the proponents of such a conception attain power, all other values are then cast to the winds. The new rulers may even pride themselves on their dedication to Justice, despite the enormous human costs in other terms. It is a melancholy but familiar story.

In fact, the question of Utopian Justice in this sense is almost the perfect model of an ethical "puzzle." The issue is posed in abstraction from any particular social setting: all the relevant facts are supposed to have long since come in. (Indeed on the Platonic conception one does not need any facts at all.) The task is to arrive clear headedly at the appropriate (simple) distributional criterion. Previous defeats and disasters only make the problem more tempting (fanatics know the same history as the rest of us; they just draw different conclusions from it), or make it seem more urgent.

Utopian Justice is unattainable. And it is not unattainable because the world is too corrupt, or too imperfect, or because Justice is a puzzle that is too hard for anyone but God. Instead the puzzle itself is incoherent. There is and can be no single formula—not even a set of lexically ordered and still vague principles like Rawls's—for Justice. This is the lesson of the pluralism that I have insisted on from the start of this book.[36] A great many values bear upon the actual institutions under which we live. The varieties of justice are among them (and they are already plural themselves) but certainly do not exhaust them. Therefore our task will always be to integrate and balance these values in the design (or rather, constant redesign) of those specific institutions I have called "middle-level."

I do not mean that we therefore cannot speak of injustice, even in very strong ways. To speak of injustice does not commit us to a single criterion of Justice, or to any utopianism at all. It is only to point out, forcefully, certain fairly gross failures, failures that we can recognize without an entire careful balancing of all of our values. The next step seems small: supposing that we know what "the" Just alternative would be. But that step is in fact a huge one and has no warrant. Even the poorest chess player can recognize that certain moves are wrong without knowing what the "right" move is; and of course there is seldom any *single* "right" move anyway.

Justice with a small "j"—and more important, what we should do all things considered—is no puzzle. It is far more difficult and less conclusive than that. We must resist the search for an abstract criterion that pulls us out of our actual problematic situations. For pragmatism the question is always simply: How can we do better? Not, What would be perfect? but simply, How can things be improved? What should we try next? There is always something to try—usually many things at once—but it is never final and complete in itself. New and unforeseen problems always open up again. The key virtue is not somehow dedication—impatient for the puzzle to be solved so that one can put the "solution" into effect—but rather the simple honesty and humility that expects to have to make more adjustments in an already-complex set of institutions tomorrow. That itself is a profound challenge. And a good deal less melancholy than the actual history of Justice.

Chapter 7
Conclusion

THIS BOOK deliberately focuses on practical issues, since it is there, naturally enough, that pragmatism stakes its claim. By way of conclusion, however, we must at least briefly take up certain more general and (it seems) inevitable concerns about a pragmatic approach to ethics. One is the objection that pragmatic methods are unacceptably "relativistic." I shall address this as "the question of critical standpoint." The other is the objection that pragmatic methods are naively optimistic. I contest both charges—briefly, summarily, and in a mood that is itself partly reconstructive rather than just reactive. The place for detailed response is elsewhere. Here there is room only to outline some responses and to question just how serious these by now rather rote objections actually are.

The Question of Critical Standpoint

Today an enormous variety of different concerns are attached to the accusation of "relativism," to the point that the term's fitness for any careful thinking at all is dubious. Even the elementary definition of "relativism" is unclear. For some philosophers, relativism is the view that accepts the equal ultimate validity of many different and incompatible belief- or value-systems. For others, relativism is

167

the view that denies ultimate validity to *any* belief- or value-system. These are drastically different views. One imagines us in a kind of bazaar; the other in a moral desert.

The objections to relativism are also extremely varied, indeed incompatible with each other. For some philosophers, relativism is simply incoherent. For others, it is perfectly coherent but merely has unfortunate consequences. Some of those who hold the latter view, in turn, take the allegedly unfortunate consequences to "refute" relativism. Others merely take them to define the modern condition. And not everyone who takes them to define the modern condition considers the results unfortunate. Some sophisticated and provocative new views seem to embrace relativism, but whether they have anything to gain from being labeled in this old way is at the very least unclear.[1]

At the core of some of these concerns, though, is a specific and fairly clear problem. Certain ethical methods seem to make it difficult for ethical communities to criticize their own values rationally. Such criticism, the objector says, must arise from a standpoint outside the community whose values are in question. This is why Rawls speaks of finding an "Archimedean point for judging the basic structure of society" to settle "the long range aim of society irrespective of the desires and needs of its present members." Without some such standpoint, the objection concludes, we seem to be condemned to more or less the community's present status quo.

Pragmatism is subject to this charge. I have emphasized that in "integrating" values we must take our actual values as starting points. On this view, we cannot stand apart from ourselves and our communities and judge them from somewhere else. Rather than seek "Archimedean points" from which our justice values can be judged, for example, we embraced Walzer's question "What would individuals like us choose, situated as we are, sharing a culture and determined to go on sharing it?" The result, however, may seem to be that there is no way to challenge that culture itself, no way to criticize the overall shape of our values. If that culture and that shape are the only possible standpoints for criticism, they do not seem open to challenge and change themselves.[2]

It is certainly possible to respond to this objection by saying, in effect, so much the worse for us. All of the traditional "standpoints," after all, are now regarded as deficient by most ethical philosophers. Rawls has abandoned his "Archimedean" aspirations. On the other hand, the problem is a serious one. Sometimes we do need a way of getting a critical grip on certain values if we are to have a progressive and intelligent life together. We can hardly challenge racism, for instance, by appealing to racist values themselves. Walzer's "communities like ours," if they happen to be racist, will presumably choose to go on being racist. We do not want to be condemned merely to making small adjustments in the status quo. Are we really to say that we cannot go farther?

Criticism as an "Inside Job"

Pragmatism answers in a very simple way. Our chief critical resources lie *within* every community's traditions and values, even resources for radically challenging the community's prevailing values and practices themselves. Ongoing social criticism is entirely possible, but it is, as Walzer puts it, typically an "inside job."[3]

From the start I have stressed the diversity of our actual values. It is this that requires integrative strategies and opens the space for reconstruction in the first place. But it also implies that no community's values are as monolithic as the objection seems to fear. It is better to recognize that there are likely to be profound tensions within the values of any community. It is upon these tensions that criticism draws. For a variety of reasons, for example, societies seldom live up to their own standards. Italian Communist and novelist Ignazio Silone explains the origins of radical criticism in just this way. We begin, he says, simply

> by taking seriously the principles taught to us by our own educators and teachers. These principles are proclaimed to be the foundations of present-day society, but if one takes them seriously and

uses them as a standard to test society as it is organized . . . today, it becomes evident that there is a radical contradiction between the two. Our society in practice ignores these principles altogether. . . . But for us they are a serious and sacred thing . . . the foundation of our inner life. The way society butchers them, using them as a mask and a tool to cheat and fool the people, fills us with anger and indignation. That is how one becomes a revolutionary.[4]

The values evoked by this kind of criticism lie close to the center of a society's own self-conception. They may be crucial to its own self-legitimation. And it is for just this reason that criticism can appeal to them so powerfully. By contrast, values truly invoked from the "outside"—if somehow we could find an "Archimedean point"—might evoke no response at all. Even those invoked at the center do not always lead to such a radical response, but they certainly create cognitive dissonance and demand some sort of accommodation. Certainly we know that we can do better by our own values than we have so far.

Silone is speaking of values that are fairly clear. More often, probably, a society will be in tension because its values themselves are not so clear. People may differ about where the "center" really lies. Critics may even invoke certain subsets of values against others in an attempt to shift the center. Even the stock anti-relativist cases, like South African apartheid, are open to criticism in this way. Indeed, it is striking that the actual widespread and persistent dissent within such societies is seldom explored by those philosophical objectors ostensibly so concerned about its possibility. But notice for example that Afrikaner dissident Andre Brink does not appeal to any external standard to justify and understand his dissent, but instead to a reunderstanding of his own community's values: "If the Afrikaner dissident today encounters such a vicious reaction from the establishment, it is because he is regarded as a traitor to everything Afrikanerdom stands for (since apartheid has usurped for itself that definition)—whereas, in fact, the dissident is fighting to assert the most positive and creative aspects of his heritage."[5] Since part of that heritage is also shared by South Africa's external critics, we may underestimate the extent to which Brink is speaking from within. Still, for him there is never a question of "standing apart." Instead, he is careful to emphasize the argument that apartheid has *usurped* central place in a far richer and more humane tradition within which he insistently still places himself—a tradition that he struggles, from the inside, to win back.

Even when standards are fairly clear and even when society has hitherto managed more or less to live up to them, there are still tensions within our values that create a space even for the strongest criticism. Consider the question of ethics and other animals, for example, discussed in Chapter 4. On the surface, it is true, "species-ism" seems a familiar and natural practice, even essential to human culture as we know it. Here it really may seem that only criticism from an entirely external standpoint can touch us. In fact, however, the opposite is once again the case.

Truly external criticism, on the one hand, may not move us at all. On the other hand, it turns out that our own culture is not so univocally speciesist at all. Many world religions, for example, speak for the other animals. For Buddhists, humanity to animals is a necessary corollary of humanity to humans. Christianity has St. Francis and St. Hubert. Native Americans' sense of community with the other animals is becoming better appreciated. The Greeks debated the morality of slaughtering dolphins and had their own anti-vivisection societies. At Rome, despite the notorious blood-thirstiness of the carnivals, the crowds cursed Pompey for having elephants attacked by lions. "Western culture," writes Mary Midgley, "is full of such thoughts." But, she goes on,

> I do not mean that they were systematically assembled into a doc-
> trine. They were not, because there was a powerful and positive
> resistance to their being so treated on the part both of the church
> and the central rationalist tradition. They remained as isolated no-
> tions, scruples felt and communicated, but not supported by any
> official framework. But it is out of such scruples that our whole
> morality is built.[6]

The task of making them systematic has perhaps fallen to us. But then the task is once again nothing like the creation or deduction of new values from some external "standpoint." Instead, the project is another form of the by-now-familiar dynamic of integration: to discover how some of our deeply embedded "scruples" can be linked with each other and with the rest of our beliefs and experiences such that they make, or make more, social and psychological sense.

Coda

I said that I would leave the answer simple. Indeed, given the diversity of objections to relativism and the extensive literature even on the "question of critical standpoint," we have no choice. Either we engage the literature in full—out of the question in a book such as this—or else just quickly sketch an attitude toward the question as a whole, as I have done, and leave our response at that. Readers can consult a variety of full-length treatments already available, including some from more or less pragmatic points of view.[7]

I propose to conclude the discussion of critical standpoints in a rather different and more speculative vein. We might ask why this problem even comes up in the first place. Is the real problem that "internal" criticism is just not visible enough? Is there some other practical problem? Or is it that something quite different is actually at stake?

The impatient answer, naturally, is that what is at stake is exactly what seems to be at stake: the possibility of certain kinds of criticism. However, if the "possibility" we mean is a *practical* possibility, this answer seems implausible. Radical social criticism is simply not that common a practice, and when it *is* undertaken it certainly does not endear itself to most people, not even to many philosophers, since most of us most of the time are on the receiving end. I can't imagine philosophers going to the mat so often for *that*.

Arguing with supposed amoralists among ourselves is perhaps occasionally a real need, but once again comparatively rare. Usually in such cases we are not prone to argue at all. In general, the more extreme and more culturally distant the imagined amoralist becomes, the less practical the demand that we have "something to say" becomes. The amount of time that we spend arguing with cannibals or Afrikaners who favor apartheid is miniscule at best, and anyway utterly insignificant beside the time spent arguing with, say, our own children. At the very least it is unclear why having something to say in these very peculiar situations somehow should be the touchstone of ethics. Suppose that we are indeed left with "nothing to say" to cannibals. Would that be a disaster? Why?

Ultimately it seems to me that philosophical resistance to relativism arises from a source that is not practical at all. Ever since Plato, philosophers have aspired to a kind of pure knowledge that transcends persons, time, and place. In this exalted realm, arguments must be universal and presuppositionless, addressed to anyone and everyone and claiming their rational assent regardless of what else they may think or believe or even whether they in fact assent. In this sense, if one ever has "something to say" with respect to an ethical question, then one always has something (in fact, the very same thing) to say. But these aspirations are directly and insistently offended by pragmatic modes of argument, where argument is particular and culture-bound, not universal and presuppositionless, and actually does aim at practical persuasion. Thus, I think, the objection about relativism at bottom protests pragmatism's abandonment of Plato, and its "insult," so to speak, to "philosophy": that is, to philosophy on the Platonic model. This may be why, for one thing, those who make such an objection are usually so uninterested in the processes and possibilities of criticism as it actually proceeds. Ultimately, for them, the real question is not whether one *can* criticize persuasively, but whether one does so in the philosophically proper way.[8]

To the extent that the objection to relativism does arise from these Platonic aspirations, though, it also stands or falls with them. But the case for any such aspirations is no longer easy to defend or even to articulate. The pragmatic claim is that it cannot be done. If so, however, then the objection seems to be thrown back into the realm of the practical, where it hardly fares well either. Perhaps it has no real home at all. At any rate we must not allow it to masquerade as a practical objection when it is not, or allow it to go only half analyzed on the practical level because we know but do not quite say that it is really about something quite different.

I regret leaving matters on this rather negative and perhaps dogmatic note; it is not in the reconstructive spirit. But if the argument so far is correct, the fault lies not with pragmatism but with the objection itself. Either the real objection, once clearly put, invokes general philosophical aspirations that are at the very least dubious, or it is a practical objection that seems to have little basis in actual practical problems. On the practical level, again, we *can* argue when it matters. It is not clear what else should concern us.

Other variants of the problem fare no better. There is, for example, the objection that relativism implies a contradiction, namely that the same act could be both right and wrong at the same time. Taken literally, this objection is misconceived, indeed just inattentive, since the very point of relativism is that there is no "right" and "wrong" *simpliciter* for the same act to both be and not be. The traditional assumption, of course, is that there *are* such universal rights and wrongs. The point here is just that one cannot invoke such assumptions as if they do not even need to be articulated, let alone defended; and it is not at all clear how to defend them. Taken less literally, meanwhile, the objection again seems to reflect the concern that logic in some form be able to get a grip on values, which is a truly practical concern but also, once again, easily allayed. Perhaps it is time to just give the whole matter a rest.

The Question of Optimism

This book has consistently stressed that a pragmatic method requires active engagement with problematic situations. Chapter 3 proposes to reconstruct the abortion debate by expanding day care and job options, rethinking the family, and in general challenging the persistent disempowerment of women. Chapter 4 proposes to reconstruct the debate about other animals by promoting vegetarian diets and alternatives to animal experimentation. Chapter 5 argues that anti-environmental interests have distorted the debate about environmental values in ways that we must expose and change. Chapters 4 and 5 also insist that in the long run we must challenge and change those current practices that reduce natural places and other animals to just what our prejudices tell us they are. Chapter 6 argues that justice questions would be better conceived as ameliorative questions about "middle-level institutions."

All of this may seem wildly optimistic. Each of these reconstructive measures will be strongly resisted. The empowerment of women threatens many men; vegetarianism is not taken lightly by the meat industry; already-established "middle-level institutions" have their own interests and inertia. In addition, change as such is threatening. It destabilizes the old practices, challenges what is familiar, and puts some part of the established world into question without offering a secure sense of what might take its place. For all of these reasons the wholesale talk of change in the previous chapters may seem naive.

Integrative hopes may also sometimes seem naive. Do I really mean to say that the two sides in the present abortion controversy might someday make it up, acknowledging that the problematic situation is more complicated and ambiguous than either side now imagines? Does Mark Sagoff really mean to say (as suggested in Chapter 5) that corporate boards and environmentalists can cooperate in setting environmental policy? Surely it was unfair of me to disparage Utopian Justice while entertaining such utterly unrealistic hopes myself!

I confess to a certain hopefulness. I do believe that the two sides in "the" abortion controversy, for example, can come together in an integrative mood. In some places it has already happened: remember Wisconsin. Nor is the reconstruction of such questions actually such a long shot. Wholesale change is the order of the day. Despite seeming, right now, the hardest nut to crack, "the" abortion issue has taken radically different shapes in different periods. Abortion was uncontroversially legal in America until the 1860s, when the nascent American Medical Association launched a campaign against abortion as a way of consolidating its professional power over midwives and lay doctors. It was a campaign for the medical control of abortion, though, not against abortion as such, and rested primarily on appeals to women's health; hence it was supported by many feminists of the period. Then the issue vanished from the political landscape until 1962, when a woman who was pregnant with what she feared was a thalidomide-damaged baby was denied an abortion after publicly warning other mothers at risk. Later in the 1960s, conservatives *favored* abortion as a means of population control. After *Roe v. Wade* (1973) the shape of the debate changed again. Only then did it begin to take the shape we now know.[9] If (when) the French abortion-inducing drug RU-486 reaches the United States, "the" issue will again change shape overnight.

Similar arguments might be made about the other issues this book has discussed. Ethical concern about other animals was completely marginalized twenty years ago. "Environmental ethics" was only a matter of pollution control. But now in both cases some of the values involved are already in practice, and institutional means of integrating them with other concerns have proliferated. There are animal-use oversight committees in university research, entire state and federal bureaucracies for "environmental protection." Most of the reconstructive strategies suggested in Chapter 3 with respect to abortion are widely discussed in the sociological literature and are central to the platforms of national women's organizations. Again, both wholesale change and the attempt to make at least some of it intelligently integrative are the story of our times.

I would argue that it is not pragmatism but rather the other side that is truly "naive": for believing that change is somehow the

exception rather than the rule, for supposing that integrative thinking must somehow be philosophically jump-started rather than recognizing integrative efforts in a wide range of existing political and
practical institutions, and, indeed, for believing that the detachment
of its own self-proclaimed "realism" does not also have consequences in the world. The argument for the last point is this. If we
acquiesce in the failures of contemporary practices and institutions
on the grounds that we are unlikely to evolve anything better, then
of course it becomes more likely that we will *not* evolve anything
better. For example, it is partly because "realists" insist that non-
violent means of conflict resolution are pipe dreams that governments continue to invest a trillion dollars annually in arms and
armies while the world's few research institutes in alternative conflict resolution have trouble even paying their light bills. It hardly
can be said that any alternatives have been tried and found wanting.
But the a priori conviction that they are not even worth trying
remains the last word. Surely it is *that* conviction that is truly "naive," not the willingness to experiment in the smallest way with
alternatives to (in this case) one of the most massively destructive
and apocalyptically threatening of all human practices.

Or again, as Chapter 4 pointed out, it is surely naive—not to
mention unscientific—for scientists who use animals in their research to claim that there are no alternatives to using animals in this
way, while undertaking no investigation of what such alternatives
might be. Usually science's promotional literature welcomes new
challenges and pictures scientists tackling great tasks with an almost
reckless optimism: controlling fusion, recreating "life," going to
Mars. Computer programmers habitually talk as though there is
nothing that computers can't do. It is certainly odd for such habitual optimists to suddenly turn "realist" when it comes to such simple matters as using cell cultures or computer programs instead of
living animals to test drugs—especially, again, when such alternatives have barely been explored. As scientists themselves would be
quick to point out in any other case, this sort of pessimism is likely

to prove self-fulfilling. Optimism on such matters seems to be the only view compatible with science's own self-advertisement.

In my view, then, there is much to be said for hopefulness. But it must also be pointed out that hopefulness is by no means required for pragmatic engagement. Dewey himself, for one, was not necessarily an optimist in this sense, despite the popular impression.[10] He simply believed that the sorts of methods proposed here are the only intelligent sorts of methods available to us to deal with problematic situations. So we employ them. We may be surprised every time they fail, or surprised every time they succeed. But expectation is a matter of temperament, and temperaments vary. At bottom, then, pragmatism may be constituted simply by a certain kind of engaged attitude, simply by integrative and reconstructive thinking. One need not be particularly hopeful about the results.

Still, I suppose, to claim that Dewey was not an optimist may seem just too paradoxical. Thinking in these ways is usually so readily mistaken for optimism that we might as well accept the label and try to make a space for pragmatic attitudes within it. Let us call Dewey's so-called optimism "structural" optimism. Structural optimism is a kind of action, then, rather than essentially a state of mind or a style of temperament. It is simply the attempt to promote more integrated values and more tractable problems; a style of interpreting and engaging problems as problematic situations and not as mere puzzles. I suppose that even structural optimists must be "hopeful" at least in the sense that they believe that such actions are not always utterly useless. But apart from this extremely minimal kind of hopefulness it seems that hopefulness and structural optimism are simply independent of each other. It is possible to be both structurally optimistic and hopeful, or one but not the other: hopeful but inactive, or active but not necessarily hopeful. So structural optimism can hardly be called naively hopeful, since it needn't be hopeful at all.

Or perhaps we need a rather different distinction, within hopefulness itself, between the belief that things *can* change for the better and the belief that they *will*. The latter is no doubt naive, and doubly so if it leads to inaction. But pragmatism requires only hopefulness of the former sort. Is the belief that things *can* change for the better "naive"? I do not think so, not if any of the integrative and reconstructive suggestions in this book are well taken. Here, I think, pragmatism rejoins all other systems of ethics, which share a professional commitment, as it were, to making a difference for the better in the world. Pragmatism may be just a little better equipped than most to succeed.

Notes and Index

Notes

Preface

1. Carol Gilligan, *In a Different Voice* (Cambridge, Mass.: Harvard University Press, 1983). As I suggest in the last section of Chapter 2, the "care" ethics for which Gilligan is particularly well-known is distinct from her "contextualism," which ought to be better known.

2. Margaret Walker, "Moral Understandings: Alternative 'Epistemology' for a Feminist Ethics," *Hypatia* 4 (1989): 21.

3. Virginia Warren, "Feminist Directions in Medical Ethics," *Hypatia* 4 (1989): 80. "Perhaps acidly," because it is left unclear whether what one is preventing are certain kinds of ethical problems or ethics itself as we know it (or both, of course).

4. Albert Jonsen and Stephen Toulmin, *The Abuse of Casuistry* (Berkeley: University of California Press, 1988), chap. 1.

5. Bernard Williams, *Ethics and the Limits of Philosophy* (Cambridge, Mass.: Harvard University Press, 1985), p. 114. See also Kai Nielson, "On Needing a Moral Theory," *Metaphilosophy* 13 (1982): 97–116.

6. See, for example, Alasdair MacIntyre, *After Virtue* (Notre Dame, Ind.: University of Notre Dame Press, 1981).

7. As a kind of summary and confirmation of the picture I have been painting, let me offer just one quotation among many possibilities from the recent literature in philosophical ethics. This happens to be from a review by James Lindemann Nelson of Steven Sapontzis's *Morals, Reason, and Animals* in *Between the Species* 6 (1990): 197: "A major ongoing debate in

moral philosophy concerns what . . . might be called the (in)Significance of Moral Theory. Influential writers . . . have raised considerable doubts about the philosophical enterprise of 'grounding' ethics in moral theory, especially if that is taken to mean one which claims to be able to derive our moral duties from a small number of basic principles. Although the critics' reasons for inveighing against the 'standard' conception of ethical theory exhibit the variety for which philosophy is (in)famous, the combined force of their work has been to put apologists for theory's traditional pretensions somewhat on the defensive. The critics' positive views about the form of moral philosophy *sans* moral theory, however, have been even more varied (and rather vaguer) than their critiques. From the lack of an articulate positive program . . . , the theorists have taken heart."

8. See Dewey's own *Theory of Valuation* (Chicago: University of Chicago Press, 1939; reprint, 1966) and James Gouinlock's useful collection, *The Moral Writings of John Dewey* (New York: Hafner Press, 1976).

9. I have sketched such a view in "Toward the Reconstruction of Subjectivism," *Journal of Value Inquiry* 18 (1984): 181–94; and "Subjectivism and the Question of Social Criticism," *Metaphilosophy* 16 (1985): 57–65.

Chapter 1
Practical Ethics in a New Key

1. Peter Singer, *Practical Ethics* (New York: Cambridge University Press, 1979). I might add that I avoid the more popular term "applied ethics" because it begs the very question that Dewey makes central: Can "theory" or "principle" somehow be prior to "practice" in ethics? (Or anywhere?) If one thinks not, then the phrase "*applied* ethics" is an inaccurate and misleading description of our actual practice.

2. Albert Jonsen and Stephen Toulmin, *The Abuse of Casuistry* (Berkeley: University of California Press, 1988), chap. 1.

3. Bernard Williams, *Ethics and the Limits of Philosophy* (Cambridge, Mass.: Harvard University Press, 1985), p. 114.

Chapter 2
Pragmatic Attitudes

1. For an accessible introduction, see James Gouinlock, ed., *The Moral Writings of John Dewey* (New York: Hafner Press, 1976). For com-

mentary, see Gouinlock, *John Dewey's Philosophy of Value* (New York: Humanities Press, 1972). Perhaps I should emphasize that the proposed view of values does not simply identify values with (all) desires. Value becomes a particularly central, profoundly structured, and critically reconstructed subspecies of desire. See also my article "Toward the Reconstruction of Subjectivism," *Journal of Value Inquiry* 18 (1984): 181–94.

2. Gouinlock, *John Dewey's Philosophy of Value,* chap. 3, sec. 1.

3. Consider that this is exactly what even an ethical theory as venerable as Kant's requires us to do: to ask *ourselves* what we can will to be a universal law for all rational beings: "I do not . . . need any penetrating acuteness in order to discern what I have to do in order that my volition may be morally good. Inexperienced in the course of the world, incapable of being prepared for all its contingencies, I ask myself only: can I will that my maxim become a universal law?" (Kant, *Foundations of the Metaphysics of Morals* [Indianapolis, Ind.: Bobbs-Merrill, 1959], p. 19). From a pragmatic point of view, as I go on to point out, this is scandalous. No one would think for a moment of making any rational nonethical decision in this way. See Gouinlock, *Moral Writings of John Dewey,* pp. xli–xlii.

4. I discuss the philosophical abortion literature in the opening section of Chapter 3.

5. This example is my own, meant to typify a huge genre. Newer contributions to the genre attempt to offer "real-life" cases (though whether anything so briefly described can be said to be "real-life" is debatable) and cases with interesting plot variations. On the general use of cases such as these as the material of ethics, see also Chapter 6 of this book. For examples of such cases, see Tom Beauchamp and James Childress, *Principles of Biomedical Ethics* (New York: Oxford University Press, 1983); or, more recently, Carol Levine, *Case Studies in Bioethics: Selections from the Hastings Center Report* (New York: St. Martin's, 1989).

6. For a full argument for this claim, see my article "Toward a Social Critique of Bioethics," *Journal of Social Philosophy* 12 (1991): 109–18.

7. For this way of putting things, see Beauchamp and Childress, *Principles of Biomedical Ethics,* Chapters 3 and 5.

8. Marvin Levine, *Effective Problem Solving* (Englewood Cliffs, N.J.: Prentice Hall, 1988), pp. 75–80; and Edward de Bono, *Lateral Thinking* (New York: Harper and Row, 1970).

9. John McKinlay opens his article "A Case for Refocussing Upstream: The Political Economy of Illness" (in *The Sociology of Health and*

Illness, ed. Peter Conrad and Rochelle Kern [New York: St Martin's, 1986]) by discussing Zola's analogy as Zola advanced it in a 1970 speech to the United Ostomy Association.

10. It might be argued that, as important as this task is, it is not the task of bioethics properly speaking. I address this defense in "Toward a Social Critique of Bioethics." In any case, even if bioethics proper has other tasks, surely ethics generally must give such questions central place.

11. Virginia Warren, "Feminist Directions in Medical Ethics," *Hypatia* 4 (1989): 79.

12. John Dewey, "The Construction of Good," chap. 10 of *The Quest for Certainty,* reprinted in Gouinlock, *Moral Writings of John Dewey,* p. 154.

13. John Dewey, *Human Nature and Conduct,* in Gouinlock, *Moral Writings of John Dewey,* pp. 141–42.

14. This is one reason why Dewey's title "The Construction of Good" is particularly well chosen.

15. I do not mean that we might not feel *regret.* A kind of regret is almost inevitable once we come to recognize how many values are at stake to which we cannot, or cannot fully, respond. But regret is not the same as guilt or the chagrin that comes with knowing that we have somehow failed. The best we might be able to do in such situations is to partially satisfy certain values. In a sense, the task of ethics is simply to figure out which losses are the least bad, which regrets the most honorable. We must not deny that really hard choices really are hard.

16. Consider these lines from a philosopher who for the moment will go unnamed: "To say that a decision is 'nothing but' a manifestation of one's preferences is to speak with little discernment. It is certainly not a matter of becoming introspectively aware of one's present attitudes—for when a decision is required those attitudes have no definite direction. Rather, it is a matter of systematizing one's actual and latent attitudes in a way which *gives* them definite direction." The sentiment is precisely Deweyan, and the point is a vital one. Desire has a certain fluidity; action is never simply an "effect" with no implications for future desire. The author, though, is Charles Stevenson, who is not usually classified as a pragmatist at all but instead as an "emotivist" in the Ayer tradition, suggesting a rather dismissive and simplified view of the affective life. Perhaps it is time to reclaim Stevenson for a different tradition. At any rate, he does write insightfully about the dynamics of values. He points out, for example, that

even an emotivist conception of values makes more facts relevant to ethical choice than its objectivist competitors do. Objectivist views tend to concentrate on *one* factor—pleasure, rights, or the like—and so lead us to think that this one factor is *all* that is relevant. But, says Stevenson, "the considerations relevant to resolving a conflict are of far greater variety." At another point he writes that *so* many factual issues are relevant that it must be left an entirely open question whether or how closely values would converge if people actually agreed about the facts. See Stevenson, *Ethics and Language* (New Haven, Conn.: Yale University Press, 1944), pp. 132–38 (the first quotation above is from p. 132); and Stevenson, "The Emotive Conception of Ethics and Its Cognitive Implications," in *Readings in Ethical Theory*, ed. Wilfrid Sellars and John Hospers (New York: Appleton-Century-Crofts, 1970), pp. 274–75.

17. There is a certain appeal, of course, in the more radical picture Sartre paints. A pragmatic picture looks more ordinary, less open to grand gestures. Sartre points out that if the young man went to a collaborationist priest, or to a friend in the Resistance, we could be pretty sure that he had already chosen his way. Oddly, though, Sartre does not consider that by coming to *him* the young man was also choosing a way, since the young man surely knew that Sartre would second his "radical" construction of the choice rather than challenge and complicate it. Perhaps by a kind of "existential choice" he had already narrowed his options to existential choices. Perhaps—but then it is that grandiosity that he needs to be talked out of.

18. Another kind of ethical holism is proposed by Morton White in his *What Is and What Ought to Be Done* (New York: Oxford University Press, 1981). White's general project is to apply to values the Quinean idea that we do not "test" isolated, individual statements against experience but instead test bodies or conjunctions of such statements. These bodies of statements, says White, often include value statements as well as factual statements, so that if "experience" (our moral reaction to certain possibilities, say) is, as Quine puts it, "recalcitrant" on some occasion, we have the option of either altering some of the factual statements or of altering some of the value statements at stake.

This kind of holism seems more congenial to pragmatism than does Rawls's holism. Certainly it avoids the presupposition that ethical thinking and criticism must of necessity be theoretical and all-inclusive. White has in mind a much more particular and ongoing process. Historically, White's view also reflects the pragmatists' insistence on the permeability of the borders between "fact" and "value," while putting the argument in the dominant analytic idiom.

But difficulties with White's view also arise from the same source. The same points can be made without thinking so exclusively of *statements*. Language has no monopoly on the dialectics of values. Furthermore, the relative formality of White's account of ethical thinking suggests that the need for adjusting or rejecting values with respect to beliefs, or vice versa, is relatively episodic. On a Deweyan view the need to rethink values is constant and not at all "formal." It is not so much a matter of "testing" as a constant process of integration and reintegration. Finally, rethinking values is not so much the "testing" of the *whole* of our statements (or values, beliefs, etc.) against a kind of "experience" still supposed to stand somehow over against them, but instead draws upon the interplay and interdependence of specific values, beliefs, and so on, depending on the situation.

19. Thus, Gilligan's "contextualism"—her name for this integrative and context-sensitive kind of thinking—is a distinct issue from her "care ethics," though the two are often run together. It is contextualism in particular with which we shall be concerned.

20. Albert Jonsen and Stephen Toulmin, *The Abuse of Casuistry* (Berkeley: University of California Press, 1988), p. 34.

21. This last point is quite remarkable and bears emphasizing. The casuist did not aim to tell us exactly what to do. Rather, the aim was to set out a range of possibilities, to partially circumscribe instead of specifically determine action. The very idea of ethics as a calculus of right action is foreign to casuistry.

22. See, for example, MacIntyre, *After Virtue,* p. 46.

23. See, for example, the essays in *Theories of Cognitive Consistency,* ed. Robert Abelson (Chicago: Rand McNally, 1968).

24. Of course there are arguments for this departure: chiefly, the idea that values must somehow be "purified," or perhaps even generated in some special way, before they can be integrated or even taken seriously in the first place. I return to some of these issues in the first part of Chapter 7. Actually, though, even if this argument were correct, integrative skills would still be necessary on any view that countenanced more than one genuine kind of value. Harmonizing our "prima facie duties" on a view like W. D. Ross's, for example, is an integrative skill.

Chapter 3
Rethinking the Abortion Debate

1. These arguments are taken up in detail in the next chapter.

2. Michael Tooley, "Abortion and Infanticide," in *The Rights and Wrongs of Abortion,* ed. Marshall Cohen, Thomas Nagel, and Thomas Scanlon (Princeton, N.J.: Princeton University Press, 1974).

3. See, for example, John Noonan, "An Almost Absolute Value in History," in *The Problem of Abortion,* ed. Joel Feinberg (Belmont, Calif.: Wadsworth, 1973).

4. For views that draw the line at birth, see Lucinda Cisler, "Unfinished Business: Birth Control and Women's Liberation," in *Sisterhood Is Powerful,* ed. Robin Morgan (New York: Random House, 1970); and Thomas Szasz, "The Ethics of Abortion," in *Everywoman's Guide to Abortion,* ed. Martin Ebon (Richmond Hill, Ontario: Simon and Schuster, 1971).

5. Feinberg, *The Problem of Abortion,* p. 4.

6. The denotation of a concept is that set of objects to which the concept applies. The denotation of "horse," for example, is the set of all horses. The suggested claim, then, is that set-membership is all or nothing, and is also *clear.* Either something is not a horse at all or else it is a horse *tout court.* In the evolution of horses from "pre-horses," there was a specific moment at which there was the first horse, and before it the last horselike nonhorse.

7. For some philosophical background to the argument of the last two paragraphs, see Kenton Machina, "Vague Predicates," *American Philosophical Quarterly* 9 (1972): 225–33; David Sanford, "Borderline Logic," *American Philosophical Quarterly* 12 (1975): 29–39; and Edward Smith and Douglas Medin, *Concepts and Categories* (Cambridge, Mass.: Harvard University Press, 1981).

8. The argument in this paragraph follows Jane English, "Abortion and the Concept of a Person," *Canadian Journal of Philosophy* 5 (1975): 235.

9. Let me briefly mention some related views for the sake of comparison and contrast. L. W. Sumner, in *Abortion and Moral Theory* (Princeton, N.J.: Princeton University Press, 1981), draws the line in the *middle* of pregnancy. Baruch Brody, in "On the Humanity of the Foetus," in

Abortion: Pro and Con, ed. R. L. Perkins (Cambridge, Mass.: Schenkman, 1974), wants to draw it specifically at the point at which fetal brain activity begins. Such views, of course, still "draw a line," and I have suggested that this project itself should be questioned and rejected. Daniel Callahan, in *Abortion, Law, Choice, and Morality* (New York: Macmillan, 1970), argues on developmental grounds that fetuses are "an important and valuable form of human life," not "mere tissue," but also holds that they are not yet persons. Callahan in effect draws *two* lines. Conception is apparently supposed to mark the entry of a being into *partial* personhood; then sometime after birth it enters full personhood. This is certainly an improvement, but still: why require everything from a conceptus to a newborn to fit into the same category? My view is that although two lines are better than one, no lines at all are better than any. Once again, I think that this is to take fetal development more seriously than Callahan does himself.

10. We could propose a parallel gradualism about the *end* of personhood. Medical ethicists have tried to determine exactly what criterion should be used to tell when a person has died. The death of the body, as determined for example by cessation of heartbeat, is not necessarily a good criterion, since personhood can be lost much earlier. Once again it is usually supposed not only that there is *a* single criterion, rather than multiple and perhaps somewhat independent aspects of personhood, but also that the end of personhood occurs at a specific point. But if personhood develops gradually, it surely can also decay gradually. Progressively more confused thinking, loss of memory, loss of the ability to use tools, and so on, may all accompany aging, and when enough of them become severe enough, personhood itself begins to come into question. There is no reason at all to suppose that there must be some point at which everything suddenly shifts.

Here too the assumption that we must draw a line, this time at the end of life, shapes the entire debate, usually without itself coming into view at all. In a well-known book, Charles Culver and Bernard Gert attempt to define (physical) death precisely enough to be medically useful. But their entire argument turns on the claim that there must be some sharp division between what they call "the process of dying" and "the process of disintegration." "If we regard death as a process," they argue, "then either (1) the process starts when the person is still living, which confuses the process of death with the process of dying, . . . or (2) the process of death starts when the person is no longer alive, which confuses the process of death with the process of disintegration" (*Philosophy in Medicine* [New York: Oxford University Press, 1982], p. 186). This dilemma is supposed to show that death cannot be a process at all. But in fact it only reasserts the assumption that there *is* such a discrete event, "death," separate from such processes. Otherwise we could say that death is a process that encompasses, or partly overlaps, both dying and disintegration. Thus, under the guise of acknowledging process, this argument actually does violence to it. Again we are trapped by an a priori conceptual scheme. Again we would do better to rethink our entire approach without such rigid boundaries and radical transition points in mind.

11. See, for example, Alessandra Piontelli, "Infant Observation from Before Birth," *International Journal of Psychoanalysis* 68 (1987): 453–63.

12. See the discussion in Michael Wreen, "The Possibility of Potentiality," *Bowling Green Studies in Applied Philosophy* 8 (1986); 139–54.

13. Carol Gilligan, *In a Different Voice* (Cambridge, Mass.: Harvard University Press, 1983), p. 81.

14. Mary Midgley, *Animals and Why They Matter* (Athens: University of Georgia, 1983), chap. 9; Leon Kass, *Toward a More Natural Science* (New York: Free Press, 1985), chap. 11.

15. Nanlouise Wolfe and Stephen Zunes, "A New Look at Abortion," *Friends Journal* (October 1988): 17.

16. Judith J. Thompson, "A Defense of Abortion," in Feinberg, *The Problem of Abortion.*

17. Hyman Rodman, Betty Sarvis, and Joy Walker Bonar, *The Abortion Question* (New York: Columbia University Press, 1987), pp. 144–45, 161, 184–86.

18. It may be argued that pregnancy due to rape is involuntary, whereas a woman pregnant from voluntarily undertaken intercourse bears some responsibility for the result and hence has already compromised the "control" of which I speak here, even if she took precautions. Part of Thompson's project is to show that this conclusion does not follow. At one point we are offered as an analogy a world in which "people-seeds" float about like pollen, and the question is whether you can be held responsible for a person-seed rooting in your carpet even if you have installed the very finest available screens and so on, only to have seeds float in due to a defect in the screens. Pregnancy due to rape is analogized to

being burglarized in similar circumstances. Even with carefully installed antiburglar bars, sometimes a burglar gets in. In either case someone might think that you are responsible anyway. After all, you left the windows open, or you kept a carpet, even though you also invested in protection. Thompson argues that you are not responsible ("Defense of Abortion," pp. 131–2). See also n. 35 below.

19. Catharine MacKinnon, "Privacy Versus Equality," in *Feminism Unmodified* (Cambridge, Mass.: Harvard University Press, 1987); Thompson, "Defense of Abortion"; and Sara Ruddick, *Maternal Thinking* (New York: Ballantine, 1989).

20. Kristin Luker, *Abortion and the Politics of Motherhood* (Berkeley: University of California Press, 1984), chap. 5 and pp. 175–86.

21. Daniel Maguire, *Abortion: A Guide to Making Ethical Choices* (Washington, D.C.: Catholics for a Free Choice, 1983); see also Roger Paynter, "Life in the Tragic Dimension," in *The Ethics of Abortion,* ed. R. M. Baird and Stuart Rosenbaum (Buffalo, N.Y.: Prometheus, 1989).

22. "A complete view of abortion," claims L. W. Sumner, "one that answers the main moral questions posed by the practice of abortion, is an ordered compound of three elements: an account of the moral status of the fetus, which grounds an account of the moral status of abortion, which in turn grounds a defense of abortion policy." ("Abortion," in *Health Care Ethics,* ed. Donald Vandeveer and Tom Regan [Philadelphia: Temple University Press, 1987], p. 164). For pragmatism, by contrast, *no* account of abortion grounded merely in "an account of the moral status of the fetus" can begin to claim to be "complete." The claim is astonishing and indeed arrogant, though the arrogance is hardly just Sumner's.

23. Gilligan, *In a Different Voice,* p. 86.

24. Luker, *Abortion and the Politics of Motherhood,* pp. 198–99.

25. In Chapter 6 I discuss and criticize Lawrence Kohlberg's theory of moral development, which is also based on interview results. A critical point not made there relates to the point made here. Kohlberg uses only hypothetical moral dilemmas in his research, not real cases, so that, for one thing, his subjects never get the chance to reconsider their judgments of the dilemmas as a result of learning from the consequences of those judgments. Their judgments *have* no consequences. This is another reason to prefer Gilligan's methods.

26. Rosalind Petchesky, "Abortion Politics in the 90s," *Nation* 250:21 (May 28, 1990): 732.

27. See Beth Maschinot, "Compromising Positions," *In These Times* 10:3 (November 20–26, 1985): 4. Since when has any abortion legislation been *unanimous*? And since when has any such legislation been *experimental*? This bill's sponsor himself calls it a "social experiment," and certain of its provisions have built-in limits. If they don't work, they expire.

28. One game used to train people in conflict resolution sets up two individuals or teams to compete for the same supply of a given good, say oranges. So focused is each side on beating out the other that they may never notice that they actually need different parts of the oranges, so that by sharing the oranges they both can achieve their goals. The situation seems "zero-sum," to use the game-theoretic term (i.e., it seems as though what one side gains, the other must lose), simply because we are not in the habit of looking for other ways out.

29. Luker, *Abortion and the Politics of Motherhood*, p. 193.

30. The last point, for instance, suggests one source of profound tension: the autonomy of women, and in particular the sexual autonomy of women, is deeply threatening to some people. There are also racial divisions cutting across the usual pro-choice/pro-life divisions. People of color have not notably supported either side. Rosalind Petchesky analyzes this phenomenon in some intriguing ways in her *Abortion and Women's Choice* (Boston: Northeastern University Press, 1990), especially chap. 4.

31. Ron Harris, "Experts Say Childhood Enduring Deep Change," *Raleigh News and Observer*, 13 May 1991, p. 5A.

32. According to a study by the Alan Guttmacher Institute as reported in *U.S. News and World Report* 105:15 (October 17, 1988): 15. That the other half did use birth control and still got pregnant also underlines the pressing need for better contraception.

33. Karen Gustafson ("The New Politics of Abortion," *Utne Reader*, [March/April 1989]: 20) reports that fewer than half of Minnesota's high schools offer any form of sex education because school officials fear the wrath of pro-lifers. See also Kristin Luker, *Taking Chances: Abortion and the Decision Not to Contracept* (Berkeley: University of California Press, 1975).

34. Recall for example the discussion of Judith Thompson's apartment analogy in n. 18 above.

35. MacKinnon, *Feminism Unmodified*, p. 95. This is why Thompson's analogies are in a way deeply insulting, even though she means them to vindicate a woman's right to abortion. For one thing, they are markedly

class-relative. Poor women have few socially enforced rights either over their own bodies or over apartments or houses, and are systematically denied the means to protect themselves or their homes even when they supposedly are granted the right. Living in a culture in which, for whole classes of women, sex *is* rape—as MacKinnon would put it—is not like once or twice having your jewelry stolen by burglars who break in when you're gone.

36. Kay Castonguay, president of Feminists for Life of Minnesota, quoted in Gustafson, "New Politics of Abortion," p. 21.

Chapter 4
Other Animals

1. Jim Mason and Peter Singer, *Animal Factories* (New York: Crown, 1980); Sidney Gendin, "The Use of Animals in Science," in *Animal Sacrifices,* ed. Tom Regan (Philadelphia: Temple University Press, 1986): and for updates, Richard Ryder, *Animal Revolution: Changing Attitudes Toward Speciesism* (Oxford: Basil Blackwell, 1989).

2. Peter Singer, *Animal Liberation* (New York: Avon, 1975), pp. 7–10 and passim; Singer, *Practical Ethics* (New York: Cambridge University Press, 1979), chap. 3.

3. See my article "Radio Astronomy as Epistemology," in *Monist* 70 (1987): 88–100.

4. Mary Midgley, *Beast and Man* (Ithaca, N.Y.: Cornell University Press, 1978), chaps. 7 and 10.

5. On the language issue in general, see ibid., chap. 10; Midgley, *Animals and Why They Matter* (Athens: University of Georgia Press, 1983), chap. 5; and Eugene Linden, *Silent Partners: The Legacy of the Ape Language Experiments* (New York: Ballantine, 1986). In *The Case for Animal Rights* (Berkeley: University of California Press, 1983), chap. 2, Tom Regan analyzes some particularly subtle versions of the speciesist appeals to language.

6. See Midgley, *Beast and Man,* chap. 11.

7. There are others; in fact, some are in a key more congenial to pragmatism, though perhaps for this very reason they are less visible than Singer's and Regan's: Midgley's *Animals and Why They Matter,* for example, and Stephen Clark's *The Moral Status of Animals* (Oxford: Clarendon

Press, 1977), both unsystematic, particular analyses of a variety of arguments and human evasions on the subject of other animals, both tending toward a vision of what Clark describes (p. 189) as "a cooperative, communicative assembly of living creatures each of its kind."

8. Singer, *Animal Liberation,* chap. 1; and *Practical Ethics,* chap. 3.

9. Regan, *Case for Animal Rights,* chaps. 7–9.

10. Ibid., pp. 267–68.

11. Singer, *Practical Ethics,* chap. 4.

12. Regan, *Case for Animal Rights,* pp. 243–47.

13. Regan rejects Singer's utilitarianism not because suffering is somehow morally irrelevant but because utilitarianism is an inadequate account of its moral relevance. See Regan, "Utilitarianism, Vegetarianism, and Animal Rights," in *All That Dwell Therein: Animal Rights and Environmental Ethics* (Berkeley: University of California Press, 1982). I return to this point at the beginning of the next section.

14. Singer, *Practical Ethics,* p. 20.

15. Regan argues that this principle, strictly applied, may not have anything like the strong implications Singer draws from it. See *Case for Animal Rights,* pp. 218–28. I think that this criticism suggests that the spirit of Singer's egalitarianism is far more important than the "letter"—a point I go on to try to make in the text in a somewhat different way.

16. For a related view of acknowledgment, though with respect to other persons, see Part 4 of Stanley Cavell, *The Claim of Reason* (New York: Oxford University Press, 1979).

17. See Regan, *Case for Animal Rights,* pp. 208–11.

18. Ibid., p. 243.

19. We may of course speak of animal "rights" more loosely. The invocation of rights might then become a kind of shorthand for the assertion that we need to take other animals more seriously, or that some proposed treatment of animals is simply intolerable, whether they are personlike or not. This is unobjectionable, I think, as long as the use of rights language as rhetorical shorthand does not mislead us into thinking that a conventional rights-argument must then be offered. There is more discussion of this point in my essay "Before Environmental Ethics," forthcoming in *Environmental Ethics* 14 (1992).

20. I am grateful to Tom Regan for conversations that have greatly clarified these points for me. I don't mean that Regan agrees with them.

21. J. Baird Callicott, "Animal Liberation: A Triangular Affair," in *People, Penguins, and Plastic Trees,* ed. Donald Vandeveer and Christine Pierce (Belmont, Calif.: Wadsworth, 1986), p. 196.

22. Singer, *Animal Liberation,* pp. 19–22, 75–76.

23. Paul Shepard, *Thinking Animals* (New York: Viking, 1978).

24. "A bird flying across the sky is an idea coming from the unseen of the preconscious and disappearing again into the realm of dreams" (ibid., p. 35). A caged bird is a model for self-understanding too, no doubt, but for a very different kind. What a dead bird on the dinner table symbolizes one wouldn't like to think.

25. For some possible "middle" views, see Rebecca Dresser, "Standards for Animal Research: Looking at the Middle," *Journal of Medicine and Philosophy* 13 (1988): 123–43; and Strachan Donnelly, "Speculative Philosophy, the Troubled Middle, and the Ethics of Animal Experimentation," *Hastings Center Report* (March/April 1989): 15–21.

26. It might be argued that however reasonable this view of things seems in calm moments, it is an unwise strategy in practice. It tends to sap moral fervor ("the person who can see all sides of the argument can never be a revolutionary") and it offers an inadequate counterweight to prevailing practice, which is left with the escape route of also presenting itself as a reasonable compromise between competing values. There is something in this objection. At the very most, though, it implies only that a less "compromising" view should be adopted as a rhetorical strategy, nothing more. We should not try to *think* in such terms. Moreover, in many settings there is no reason that one cannot uncompromisingly insist on the need to take certain values more seriously. This is not the same as making them bear the entire weight.

27. These points are further developed in the concluding sections of this chapter and the next, and in my "Before Environmental Ethics."

28. See "Vegetarian Diets," a technical support paper outlining the position of the American Dietetic Association, *Journal of the American Dietetic Association* 88 (March 1988): 351–52; and John Robbins, *Diet for a New America* (Walpole, N.H.: Stillpoint, 1987).

29. Andrew Rowan, *Alternatives to Laboratory Animals* (Washington, D.C.: Institute for the Study of Animal Problems, 1980); and Dallas Pratt, *Alternatives to Pain in Experiments on Animals* (New York: Argus Archives, 1980).

30. Lawrence Finsen, "Institutional Animal Care and Use Committees," *Journal of Medicine and Philosophy* 13 (1988): 145–58.

31. Shepard might ask: What is the unconscious message to children when the dead bodies of animals are all that their education brings them into contact with?

32. Midgley, *Animals and Why They Matter,* p. 115.

33. Midgley, *Beast and Man,* pp. 229–30. A nice counterpoint to this story is told in Sy Montgomery, *Walking with the Great Apes* (Boston, Houghton Mifflin, 1991), pp. 265–66: "Once Geza Teleki [one of Jane Goodall's co-workers at Gombe] found himself in exactly this position [the position of Kohler's chimps]. He had followed the chimpanzees down into the valley and around noon discovered that he had forgotten to bring his lunch. The chimps were feeding on fruit in the trees at the time, and he decided to try to knock some fruit from nearby vines with a stick. For about ten minutes he leaped and swatted with his stick but didn't manage to knock down any fruit. Finally an adolescent named Sniff collected a handful of fruit, came down the tree, and dropped the fruit into Geza's hands."

34. Konrad Lorenz, *King Solomon's Ring: New Light on Animals' Ways* (New York: Time, 1962); Vicki Hearne, *Adam's Task: Calling Animals by Name* (New York: Knopf, 1986); and Jim Nollman, *Dolphin Dreamtime: The Art and Science of Interspecies Communication* (New York: Bantam, 1987).

Chapter 5
The Environment

1. The main argument for the Shoreham nuclear power plant on Long Island was that its generating capacity was necessary to meet the peak demand, which occurs in the summer. Forty percent of that peak demand is for air conditioning. On patterns of and potential changes in energy use in general, see Amory Lovins, *Soft Energy Paths* (San Francisco: Friends of the Earth International, 1977); and Lester Brown, Christopher Flavin, and Sandra Postel, "A Sensible Energy Strategy," *Multinational Monitor* (January/February 1989): 14–16. For a detailed discussion of the ethical issues raised here, see Richard and Val Routley, "Nuclear Power:

Some Ethical and Social Dimensions," in *And Justice for All: New Introductory Essays in Ethics and Public Policy,* ed. Tom Regan and Donald Vandeveer (Totowa, N.J.: Rowman and Allanheld, 1982); and K. S. Shrader-Frechette, *Nuclear Power and Public Policy* (Dordrecht, Neth.: Reidel, 1983).

2. Holmes Rolston III, *Philosophy Gone Wild* (Buffalo, N.Y.: Prometheus Books, 1986), p. 137.

3. Aldo Leopold, "Some Fundamentals of Conservation in the Southwest," *Environmental Ethics* 1 (1979): 138.

4. Christopher Stone, *Should Trees Have Standing? Toward Legal Rights for Natural Objects* (Los Altos, Calif.: Kaufmann, 1974).

5. The view developed in the pages to follow, for example, is rooted in a subjectivist theory of values but is not anthropocentric. Indeed, I argue that the entire distinction between anthropocentric and nonanthropocentric views ought to be pushed overboard. More generally, a subjectivist view of values only roots the process of *valuation* in valuers. It says nothing at all about what they may actually value. Even if valu*ing* is something that only humans do, it still would not follow that only humans have value. For a discussion of similar points in somewhat different terms, see Kelley Parker, "The Values of a Habitat," *Environmental Ethics* 12 (1990): 353–68; L. W. Sumner, "Subjectivity and Moral Standing," *Bowling Green Studies in Applied Philosophy* 8 (1986): 1–15; and Richard and Val Routley, "Against the Inevitability of Human Chauvinism," in *Ethics and Problems of the 21st Century,* ed. Kenneth Goodpaster and Kenneth Sayre (Notre Dame, Ind.: University of Notre Dame Press, 1979), pp. 36–59.

6. Tom Regan, "The Nature and Possibility of an Environmental Ethic," *Environmental Ethics* 3 (1981): 30–34.

7. G. E. Moore, *Philosophical Studies* (London: Paul, Trench, Tubner, 1922), p. 260. Regan himself avoids the terminology of "intrinsic" value because it seems to him to be contaminated by its peculiar employment by hedonistic utilitarians, for whom only pleasure is good in itself and actual sentient beings become only "receptacles" for such intrinsic values, not good in themselves. See Tom Regan, *The Case for Animal Rights* (Berkeley: University of California Press, 1983), pp. 235–36. But the Moorean sense of the notion of intrinsic value proposed here, and widespread in environmental ethics, is rarely utilitarian, and so at least does not seem to have *this* problem.

8. G. E. Moore, *Principia Ethica* (Cambridge: Cambridge University Press, 1971), p. 187.

9. J. Baird Callicott, "Nonanthropocentric Value Theory and Environmental Ethics," *American Philosophical Quarterly* 21 (1984): 304.

10. Alasdair MacIntyre, *After Virtue* (Notre Dame, Ind.: Notre Dame University Press, 1981), chap. 2.

11. Peter Singer, *Animal Liberation* (New York: Avon, 1975), pp. 176–82; Mark Sagoff, "Nature and the National Idea," in his *Economy of the Earth* (New York: Cambridge University Press, 1988); and Thomas Hill, Jr., "Ideals of Human Excellence and Preserving Natural Environments," *Environmental Ethics* 6 (1983): 211–24.

12. Bryan Norton, "Environmental Ethics and Weak Anthropocentrism," *Environmental Ethics* 6 (1984): 131–48. For an example of the tendency to invoke intrinsic values as "givens" in the sense described, see James Anderson, "Moral Planes and Intrinsic Values," *Environmental Ethics* 13 (1991): 49–58.

13. Jim Cheney, "Eco-feminism and Deep Ecology," *Environmental Ethics* 9:2 (1987): 115–45.

14. In "Beyond Intrinsic Value: Pragmatism in Environmental Ethics," *Environmental Ethics* 7 (1985): especially 324–27.

15. Holmes Rolston III, "Are Values in Nature Subjective or Objective?" in *Philosophy Gone Wild,* p. 112.

16. Richard Routley, "Is There a Need for a New, an Environmental, Ethic?" in *Proceedings of the Fifteenth World Congress in Philosophy* (Sofia: World Congress in Philosophy, 1973), pp. 205–10. Rolston suggests something similar in "Are Values in Nature Subjective or Objective?" p. 114.

17. This terminology may be found in Arne Naess, "The Shallow and the Deep, Long-Range Ecology Movements: A Summary," *Inquiry* 16 (1973): 95–100. See also Bill Devall and George Sessions, *Deep Ecology* (Layton, Utah: Peregrine Smith Books, 1984).

18. A variety of other criticisms of the appeal to intrinsic values have been offered by myself and others in a variety of places. A number of further criticisms are contained in my article "Beyond Intrinsic Value" and in "Between Means and Ends," forthcoming in *Monist* (1992). Tom Regan's views a decade after "The Nature and Possibility of an Environmental Ethic" can be found in "Does Environmental Ethics Rest on a Mis-

take?" also forthcoming in *Monist* (1992). This piece is a sharp attack on the ontology of supposed intrinsic values in nature. Some holistic objections to the individualism of the concept of intrinsic value can be found in Eric Katz, "Searching for Intrinsic Value," *Environmental Ethics* 9 (1987): 235–36.

19. Holmes Rolston III, "The Human Standing in Nature: Storied Fitness in the Moral Overseer," *Bowling Green Studies in Applied Philosophy* 8 (1986): 95ff.

20. Aldo Leopold, *Sand County Almanac* (New York: Oxford University Press, 1949). From the present point of view it is unfortunate that "The Land Ethic" essay is so often reprinted alone elsewhere. Leopold himself located it much more wisely, much more "ecologically." For further discussion, see John Rodman, "Four Forms of Ecological Consciousness Reconsidered," in *Ethics and the Environment,* ed. Donald Scherer and Thomas Attig (Englewood Cliffs, N.J.: Prentice Hall, 1983), pp. 88–92.

21. Rolston, "Human Standing in Nature," p. 96.

22. See my essay "Forms of Gaian Ethics," *Environmental Ethics* 9 (1987): 217–30.

23. Holmes Rolston III, "Values Gone Wild," in *Philosophy Gone Wild,* p. 122.

24. Leopold, *Sand County Almanac,* pp. 224–25.

25. Bryan Norton, "Conservation and Preservation: A Conceptual Rehabilitation," *Environmental Ethics* 8 (1986): 220.

26. Ibid., p. 213.

27. Ibid., 218. For a related proposal, forms of which have appeared in both *Earth First! Journal* and the mainline environmental management literature, see Reed Noss and Larry Harris, "Nodes, Networks, and MVMS: Preserving Diversity at All Scales," *Environmental Management* 10 (1986): 299–309.

28. Dave Foreman, "Dreaming Big Wilderness," *Wild Earth* 1 (1991): 10–13. See also "The Earth First! Wilderness Preserve System," *Wild Earth* 1 (1991): 33–38.

29. John B. Judis, "Ancient Forests, Lost Jobs," *In These Times* 14:31 (August 1–14, 1990): 8. See also "Owl Versus Man" (a title somewhat belied even by this rather mainstream article), *Time* (June 25, 1990): 56–62.

30. "The Politics of Posterity," *Economist* 312 (September 2, 1989): 4.

31. Paul Mohai, "Public Concern and Elite Involvement in Conservation Issues," *Social Science Quarterly* 66 (1985): 820–38.

32. Denton Morrison and Riley Dunlap, "Environmentalism and Elitism: A Conceptual and Empirical Analysis," *Environmental Management* 10 (1986): 583 and passim: a fine discussion in general.

33. For a general discussion, see Keith Davis and Robert Blomstrom, *Business and Society: Environment and Responsibility,* 3d ed. (New York: McGraw-Hill, 1975).

34. One can still also ask about how to decide in cases where the choice really *is* "owls versus man" or the like, and the answer is of some philosophical interest and at least sometimes also of practical interest. One can also ask how to persuade the truly least persuadable to, say, care about snail darters. But again, I am arguing that these are emphatically *not* the central questions we face, at bottom, either ethically or politically, and we do ourselves a disservice, distracting attention and energy from more important and more promising questions, if we carry on as though they are.

35. Amory Lovins, in "The Negawatt Revolution," *Across the Board* (September 1990): 18–23; reprinted in *Environment 91/92*, ed. John Allen (Guilford, Conn.: Dushkin, 1991), pp. 111–16, argues that three-fourths of the electricity Americans currently consume can be saved, and in ways that will stimulate the economy. On the unaccounted-for ecological costs of new energy development, see Walter Rosenbaum, *Energy, Politics, and Public Policy* (Washington, D.C.: Congressional Quarterly, 1981), chap. 4; and Thomas H. Lee, Ben C. Ball, and Richard Tabors, *Energy Aftermath* (Boston: Harvard Business School Press, 1990), chap. 5, especially pp. 143–48.

36. See Shrader-Frechette, *Nuclear Power and Public Policy,* chap. 3. Fossil fuels also have vast and unaccounted-for costs: for example, the costs of the wars, naval escorts for convoys, and so on, that characterize American relations with the major oil-producing region of the world.

37. Even DuPont, which resisted for years, is coming around. See "New DuPont Line," *New York Times,* 22 January 1991, p. D4, and "DuPont to Stop Emissions of a Gas," 8 March 1991, p. D3.

38. Mark Sagoff, "The Greening of the Blue Collars," *Report from the Institute for Philosophy and Public Policy* 10 (1990): 5.

39. This is argued in some detail in my essay "Before Environmental Ethics," forthcoming in *Environmental Ethics* 14 (1992).

40. My current and projected work is heading in these directions.

Chapter 6
Justice

1. Lawrence Kohlberg, "Stage and Sequence: The Cognitive-Developmental Approach to Socialization," in *Handbook of Socialization Theory and Research,* ed. D. A. Goslin (Chicago: Rand McNally, 1969), p. 379.

2. Lawrence Kohlberg, "Moral Stages and Moralization," in *Moral Development and Behavior: Theory, Research, and Social Issues,* ed. Thomas Lickona (New York: Holt, Rinehart and Winston, 1976), pp. 34–35.

3. Lawrence Kohlberg, Charles Levine, and Alexandra Hemer, *Moral Stages: A Current Reformulation and Response to Critics* (Basel: Karger, 1983), pp. 92–95.

4. See Carol Gilligan, "Moral Orientation and Moral Development," in *Women and Moral Theory,* ed. Eva F. Kittay and Diana T. Meyers (Totowa, N.J.: Rowman and Littlefield, 1987), p. 21.

5. Carol Gilligan, *In a Different Voice* (Cambridge, Mass.: Harvard University Press, 1983), especially chap. 3. For a summary, see Kittay and Meyers's introduction to *Women and Moral Theory.*

6. One fundamental problem is that true longitudinal tests have not yet been possible—the model is too new—so taking the model to describe moral *development* is still rather conjectural.

7. These points are raised in Marilyn Friedman's fine commentary on the Kohlberg–Gilligan debate, "Care and Context in Moral Reasoning," in Kittay and Meyers, *Women and Moral Theory,* especially pp. 201–2.

8. In *In a Different Voice,* pp. 27–38, Gilligan analyzes a number of interview transcripts in light of Kohlberg's categories to show how these classifications emerge and confirm themselves. See also Annette Baier, "Hume: The Women's Moral Theorist?" in Kittay and Meyers, *Women and Moral Theory,* p. 39.

9. William Boyce and Larry Jensen, *Moral Reasoning: A Psychological–Philosophical Investigation* (Lincoln: University of Nebraska Press, 1978), p. 196.

10. Kohlberg, Levine, and Hemer, *Moral Stages,* p. 92.

11. Friedman, "Care and Context in Moral Reasoning," p. 199.

12. It is often claimed that moral values by nature "override" all other values, which if true would make the present claim both confused and maybe even morally suspect (supposing, at any rate, that justice or impartiality is the central *moral* virtue in turn). On the contrary, however, I believe that it is the claim of moral values to override all other values that is both confused and maybe even morally suspect. But this is a tangled debate. I touch on this matter in my essay "Toward an Inclusive Ethics," *Bowling Green Studies in Applied Philosophy* 8 (1986): 36–39. For other literature on the issue, see W. D. Falk, "Morality, Self, and Others," in *Morality and the Language of Conduct,* ed. H. N. Casteneda and G. Nakhnikian (Detroit: Wayne State University Press, 1965); Robert Brandom, "Points of View and Practical Reason," *Canadian Journal of Philosophy* 12 (1982): 321–33; and Philippa Foot, "Are Moral Considerations Overriding?" in *Virtues and Vices* (Berkeley: University of California Press, 1978).

I think the standard arguments that morality must be overriding not only fail but backfire. To say, as Kurt Baier does in *The Moral Point of View* (Ithaca, N.Y.: Cornell University Press, 1958), that morality is "set up" to be overriding only succeeds in making it fishy. Falk notes a tendency to conflate two senses of the term "morality" itself: one that essentially associates it with "our whole capacity of self-direction by good and sufficient reasons," the other invoking the much narrower business of respecting persons or doing justice. This leads to a kind of equivocation in the basic argument such that we are led to think that the same specific "moral" institution is both at once, both overriding and only concerned, say, with doing justice. It is this tendency toward equivocation (or at the very least inexplicitness), I think, that leads Foot to complain of what she calls "an element of deception in the official line about morality," and William Frankena to write that "a few of morality's defenders have concluded that being moral does not always pay the individual, and that morality should recognize this and keep quietly to its place, or else go on 'bulling it out' anyway, as it has been doing with some, if not complete success" (*Thinking About Morality* [Ann Arbor: University of Michigan Press, 1980], p. 80). These sorts of remarks are astonishing, coming from writers who are after all among the most preeminent moral philosophers writing in English. Perhaps they have given the overriders pause. One hears a good deal less from them these days.

13. See, for example, Bernard Williams, "A Critique of Utilitarianism," in *Utilitarianism For and Against,* ed. J. J. C. Smart and Bernard Williams (New York: Cambridge University Press, 1973), pp. 92–93.

14. John Rawls, *A Theory of Justice* (Cambridge, Mass.: Harvard University Press, 1971), p. 7

15. Ibid., p. 195ff.

16. Ibid., p. 137.

17. See, for example, ibid., pp. 4, 9, where Rawls claims that justice has "primacy" and that it provides "a standard whereby the distributive aspects of the basic structure of society are to be assessed." Of course, all of this is still very ambiguous. The passive structure of the last phrase, for example, makes it impossible to tell who is doing the "assessing," and whether that person or institution is just anyone, anytime, or occupies a special role into which the primacy of justice is built from the start. Once the theory has gathered steam, Rawls simply marginalizes all other values, like the environmental, historical, and cultural values just mentioned in the text. Views that would consider them he labels "ideal-regarding" (p. 326), thus neatly reducing them to various forms of a refusal to honor existing human wants. He then argues that they are excluded by structural features of the Original Position (p. 328), which of course is true but merely begs the question.

18. Currently in the United States, about forty million people have no health insurance at all, and an equal number have seriously limited coverage. See J. Robert Hunter and Gail Shearer, testimony before the House Subcommittee on Health and Long-Term Care of the House Subcommittee on Aging, reported in *Congressional Digest* 66:4 (1987): 111, 123. Even the American Medical Association has recently come around to the idea of extending guaranteed medical coverage to all.

19. For more argument along these lines, see my essay "Toward a Social Critique of Bioethics," *Journal of Social Philosophy* 12 (1991): 109–18.

20. Rawls, *Theory of Justice,* pp. 260, 263.

21. Marxist critics hold that Rawls begs the question in favor of modern liberalism and the bourgeois individualist state. Non-Marxists too object to what Thomas Nagel calls the "strong individualist bias" of the Original Position, to the highly conservative attitude toward risk taking embodied in the "maximin" principle, to the exclusion of everything except the "thinnest" conceptions of the good (an exclusion Nagel accuses not

only of not being neutral but of not even being fair), and to other features of the Original Position. Robert Nozick, for his part, holds that Rawls's presuppositions are not individualistic *enough*. See the essays collected in Norman Daniels, ed., *Reading Rawls* (New York: Basic Books, 1976). Nozick's criticism can be found in *Anarchy, State, and Utopia* (New York: Basic Books, 1974), chap. 7, part II.

22. John Rawls, "Kantian Constructivism in Moral Theory," *Journal of Philosophy* 77 (1980): 518.

23. John Rawls, "Justice as Fairness: Political Not Metaphysical," *Philosophy and Public Affairs* 14 (1985): 225, 230.

24. See Rawls, *Theory of Justice,* chap. 9.

25. Ibid., pp. 21, 48–51, 120f.

26. Not even Rawls, after all, really manages to unify all the competing relevant considerations. This too is a familiar point of criticism. Rawls, it is argued, excludes religious values, along with all other forms of "perfectionism," from the Original Position. He insists on only the most conservative strategy under uncertainty. He ignores, or at least radically reconstitutes, "entitlement." He makes "natural talents" into "common assets" in a troubling way. He allows that opportunity will never be completely fair as long as families exist, but surely does not want to abolish the family. Again, there is an entire range of such criticism—see the works cited in n. 21 above. As elaborate and complex and judicious as Rawls's theory is, the range of relevant values outstrips even him.

27. Bernard Williams, *Ethics and the Limits of Philosophy* (Cambridge, Mass.: Harvard University Press, 1985), p. 17 and passim.

28. Michael Walzer, *Spheres of Justice: A Defense of Pluralism and Equality* (New York: Basic Books, 1983), p. 5.

29. Ibid., p. 4.

30. Ibid., p. 103.

31. Christopher Stone, *Where the Law Ends: The Social Control of Corporate Behavior* (New York: Peter Smith, 1975).

32. The commonly mentioned countervailing considerations have to do with the workability and affordability of programs like Medicare. These are serious concerns, of course, but of a rather different order. One might agree, again, that some kind of communal protection against catastrophe is wise, while leaving open the question of what form it should take. When one hears a truly ethical objection it is usually by extension from a liber-

tarian principle, such as the principle that coercion for the sake of other people's good is morally wrong, to the case of tax-supported aid to others. The proper answer, I believe, is that sometimes it is wrong and sometimes it is not. The libertarian principle is not the sole principle of ethics. Everything depends on what kind of aid is in question and what the actual costs are to those who support it. This is the answer suggested by our actual practice, again; and from a pragmatic point of view it exemplifies a wisdom that we ought to respect.

33. It is still not uncommon to hear some philosophers argue that moral reasons are by definition "overriding." As I say in n. 12, I think this is an indefensible if not somewhat disingenuous claim. Let me add here only that Rawls, at any rate, may not make such a claim for justice. See *Theory of Justice*, p. 17, for instance, where he states that justice as fairness does not exhaust even all the moral virtues, let alone all moral relationships. "We must recognize the limited scope of justice as fairness and of the general type of view that it exemplifies." On the other hand, justice *is* supposed to have "primacy" over other values (see n. 17). Rawls's ultimate view on these matters remains murky.

34. Cf. Chapter 4, n. 19.

35. The latter formulation is Robert Nozick's, from *Anarchy, State, and Utopia*, p. 160. Nozick's view at least has the virtue that it defines justice in terms of the outcome of ongoing processes, as opposed to the usual formulae, which look to structural and fixed features of situations—what Nozick calls "end-state" views. Egalitarianism is the clearest, or anyway simplest, case. But Nozick's is still a formula, still insists on *one* and only one relevant type of value.

36. Walter Kaufmann reaches a similar conclusion in chap. 3 of *Without Guilt and Justice* (New York: Wyden, 1973).

Chapter 7
Conclusion

1. For a survey of various interpretations of and objections to relativism, see Jack Meiland and Michael Krausz, eds., *Relativism: Cognitive and Moral* (Notre Dame, Ind.: Notre Dame University Press, 1982). For new views that might be labeled "relativistic" but probably shouldn't be,

see Richard Bernstein, *Beyond Objectivism and Relativism* (Philadelphia: University of Pennsylvania Press, 1983); and Donna Haraway, "Situated Knowledges: The Science Question in Feminism and the Privilege of Partial Perspective," *Feminist Studies* 14 (1988): 575–99.

2. Thus, Ronald Dworkin objects sharply to Walzer's basic outlook: "It is a part of our common political life, if anything is, that justice is our critic not our mirror, that any decision about the distribution of any good . . . may be reopened no matter how firm the traditions that are then challenged, that we may always ask of some settled institutional scheme whether it is fair. Walzer's relativism is faithless to the single most important social practice we have: the practice of worrying about what justice really is" ("To Each His Own," *New York Review of Books,* 14 April 1983, p. 6). Ethics, in short, must not simply reflect what we or others do in fact value. "Justice is our critic, not our mirror." Relativism, on this view, is "faithless" to the most essential impulses of ethics itself.

3. Michael Walzer, *Interpretation and Social Criticism* (Cambridge, Mass.: Harvard University Press, 1987), chap. 2.

4. Ignazio Silone, *Bread and Wine,* trans. Gwenda David and Eric Mosbacher (New York: Harper, 1937), pp. 157–58.

5. Andre Brink, *Writing in a State of Siege: Essays on Politics and Literature* (New York: Summit Books, 1983), p. 19.

6. Mary Midgley, *Beast and Man* (Ithaca, N.Y.: Cornell University Press, 1978), p. 220.

7. Bernstein, *Beyond Objectivism and Relativism;* Sabina Lovibond, *Realism and Imagination in Ethics* (Minneapolis: University of Minnesota Press, 1983); Walzer, *Interpretation and Social Criticism* and *The Company of Critics* (New York: Basic Books, 1988).

8. Here my argument follows Dewey's general line in *The Quest for Certainty* (New York: Perigee, 1980).

9. Kristin Luker, *Abortion and the Politics of Motherhood* (Berkeley: University of California Press, 1984), chaps. 2–6. See also Nanlouise Wolfe and Stephen Zunes, "A New Look at Abortion," *Friends Journal* (October 1988): 19.

10. James Gouinlock, *John Dewey's Philosophy of Value* (New York: Humanities Press, 1972), p. 118n.

Index